WRITING POWER 1

Language Use • Social and Personal Writing • Academic Writing • Vocabulary Building

Karen Blanchard

Writing Power 1

Pearson Education, 10 Bank Street, White Plains, NY 10606

Staff credits: The people who made up the *Writing Power 1* team, representing editorial, production, design, and manufacturing, are Aerin Csigay, Dave Dickey, Nancy Flaggman, Ann France, Shelley Gazes, Penny Laporte, Amy McCormick, Liza Pleva, Massimo Rubini, and Jaimie Scanlon.

Cover images: Shutterstock.com (first 3 images), Jeffrey Coolidge/Corbis (far right image)
Text composition: TSI Graphics
Text font: 13.5/15 Adobe Caslon
Credits: See page 262

Library of Congress Cataloging-in-Publication Data
Blanchard, Karen Lourie
  Writing power. 1 : language use social and personal writing, academic writing, vocabulary building / Karen Blanchard.
    p. cm.
  ISBN 0-13-231484-3—ISBN 0-13-231485-1—ISBN 0-13-231486-X—ISBN 0-13-231487-8
  1. English language—Textbooks for foreign speakers.   2. English language—Rhetoric—
Problems, exercises, etc.   3. Report writing—Problems, exercises, etc.   I. Title.
  PE1128.B5874   2012
  428.2'4—dc23
                                                                                    2012006120

ISBN-10: 0-13-231484-3
ISBN-13: 978-0-13-231484-8

Printed in the United States of America
3 17

Contents

Acknowledgments

The author would like to acknowledge Beatrice S. Mikulecky and Linda Jeffries for their innovations in the *Reading Power* series, and the Pearson team for all of their efforts and contributions in making the *Writing Power* series a reality, especially Paula Van Ells, Amy McCormick, Massimo Rubini, and series co-authors Sue Peterson and Dorothy Zemach. A special thanks goes to development editor Jaimie Scanlon, whose keen mind and insights were invaluable in the shaping of this text.

I would also like to thank my editor and friend Penny Laporte who shared my vision for this book and whose brilliance and humor made working on this project a wonderful experience. Finally, I am grateful to my colleague Andrea Brooks, my friend Lillian Surdo, and my son Daniel for their support, encouragement, and ideas.

Writing Power 1 Reviewers:
The publisher would like to extend special thanks to the following individuals who reviewed *Writing Power* and whose comments were instrumental in developing this series.

Jeff Bette, Naugatuck Valley Community College; **Leslie Biaggi**, Miami-Dade Community College; **Linda Ciano**, American Language Institute, New York University; **Sally C. Gearhart**, Santa Rosa Community College; **Anthony Halderman**, Cuesta College, San Luis Obispo, CA; **Melissa L. Parisi**, Westchester Community College; **Jason Tannenbaum**, Pace University; **Joe Walther**, Korea

About the Author

Karen Blanchard has been in the TESOL field for thirty years. She has taught ESL at English Language programs at the University of Pennsylvania, the American Language Academy, and Gratz College. She has also taught education courses and conducted workshops in curriculum and materials development and teacher training. Her areas of specialty and interest are teaching writing and reading, academic English, testing, and language acquisition. She now concentrates on writing textbooks and designing materials to develop literacy and fluency.

Introduction to *Writing Power 1*

To the Teacher

Writing Power 1 is unlike most other writing textbooks. Rather than focusing on one area of writing, such as fluency, language use, academic writing, or social writing, *Writing Power 1* includes all of them to give students practical skills for writing in many different situations. The book is also organized in a different way. It contains four separate Parts that concentrate on four important aspects of writing proficiency; therefore it is like four books in one. The book's structure is flexible, allowing you to assign work from different sections of the book concurrently and to target your students' greatest needs.

Writing Power 1 includes four parts:

- **Part 1: Language Use**
- **Part 2: Social and Personal Writing**
- **Part 3: Academic Writing**
- **Part 4: Vocabulary Building**

Writing Power 1 is designed to meet the needs of students in intensive English and pre-college programs, college bridge programs, or college or university classes. The focus is on basic skills for successful written communication in and outside the classroom. *Writing Power 1* is intended for students at the beginning to high-beginning level.

The purpose of *Writing Power 1* is to develop students' writing skills for a variety of purposes. Exercises target both accuracy and fluency and give students the tools they need to express themselves in effective and interesting ways. Students learn appropriate vocabulary and structures for academic and social settings, as well as techniques for creative writing.

Students also work on writing fluency throughout the course, using journal and blog assignments. The Writing Power Blog can be found at **http://pearsonELT.com/ writingpowerblog**. Log on to see instructions for how to set up a private class blog, where your students can post writing assignments and communicate with classmates in a fun online environment. The Further Practice boxes throughout the book give ideas for blog assignments, as well as journal topics and research projects.

A typical unit focuses on a central topic or theme and guides students through the full writing process. Students work individually, in pairs, and in groups to:

- Brainstorm ideas
- Select, organize, and develop ideas
- Draft a text
- Check and revise the text
- "Publish" their work by sharing it with classmates and/or you

The final Writing Task at the end of the unit integrates all of the skills presented. To close the unit, students use the *Check Your Writing* checklist to review and revise their writing.

A separate Teacher's Guide contains the answer key, a rationale for the approach taken in *Writing Power 1*, specific suggestions for using it in the classroom, and a sample syllabus.

The author hopes you and your students will enjoy using *Writing Power 1*.

To the Student

Writing is an important part of academic and social life, both on paper and online. *Writing Power 1* teaches you skills to improve your writing in both of these areas. You will work on writing both fluently (quickly and easily) and accurately (correctly and appropriately).

This book is different from other writing textbooks. *Writing Power 1* is divided into four Parts. Instead of working on one part at a time, as in most books, you can and should work regularly on all four parts of the book.

Part 1: Language Use This Part helps you learn to write correctly. You will learn how to write good sentences and express your ideas about different topics in writing.

Part 2: Social and Personal Writing It is important to write as often as you can about topics you are interested in. Units such as "Emails and Blogs" and "Journals" will help you learn to write more quickly and easily in English. On the Writing Power Blog, located at **http://pearsonELT.com/writingpowerblog**, you and your classmates can post comments and have fun writing in English.

Part 3: Academic Writing In this Part, you will learn how to organize ideas and write academic paragraphs in English. You will practice writing different types of paragraphs that are common in academic assignments.

Part 4: Vocabulary Building This Part helps you find and choose useful words for your writing. You will learn ways to study and remember new vocabulary.

The author hopes you will enjoy studying with *Writing Power 1*!

Begin by taking the Writing Questionnaire on the next page.

Questionnaire

What Does Writing Mean to You?

A. *Complete this questionnaire about writing in your life.*

Questionnaire

1. What is your name? _____

2. Where are you from? _____

3. Where do you live now? _____

4. What is your first language? _____

5. Do you speak any other languages? _____

6. Do you like to write in your language? _____

7. What do you write in your language? What do you write in English?
Check (✓) your answers.

	In your language	In English
Letters		
Postcards		
Text messages		
Emails		
Blogs		
Memos		
Journals		
Other (add your own idea):		
Other (add your own idea):		

B. *Talk about your answers with another student. Are they the same?*

Language Use

Words, phrases, sentences, and paragraphs are the basic building blocks of writing. In writing, we put letters together to form words. We put words together to form phrases, and phrases together to form sentences. We put sentences together to form paragraphs. And we put paragraphs together to form essays, articles, chapters, and books. When we do this correctly, our writing is easy to understand and interesting to read.

In this unit, you will learn some important information about English sentences. Writing correct sentences is important in school as well as at work and in your everyday life.

Warm Up

A. *Look at the pictures. Read the sentences in the box. Write the correct sentences under each picture. Follow the examples.*

> ~~Nick sells cars.~~   She works hard.
> ~~Rachel is a photographer.~~ She takes pictures.
> He likes his job.   He is a salesperson.

1.

a. *Rachel is a photographer.*

b. _____

c. _____

2.

a. _Nick sells cars._

b. _____

c. _____

B. *Work with another student. Take turns. Read the sentences in Exercise A aloud.*

The sentences under each picture are complete sentences. Each one has a subject and a verb. Each sentence expresses a complete idea.

Look at this group of words:

> *Nick sells cars.*

This is a sentence.
It has a subject (*Nick*).
It has a verb (*sells*).

Look at this group of words:

> *Sells cars*

This is not a sentence.
It does not have a subject.

Now look at this group of words:

> *Nick cars*

This is not a sentence.
It does not have a verb.

PARTS OF A SENTENCE

The main parts of a sentence are the subject and the verb. Many sentences also have an object or other information after the verb. An English sentence begins with a capital letter. It ends with a period (.), question mark (?), or exclamation point (!).

What Is the Subject?

The **subject** tells *who* or *what* the sentence is about. It is usually at the beginning of the sentence. The subject is usually a noun or a pronoun. (A noun is a person, place, or thing.) The subject can be one word or more than one word. Look at the underlined subjects in the examples.

Examples:

<u>Scott</u> drives a bus.

<u>The bus</u> stops at every corner.

<u>Marta and Oscar</u> take the bus to work.

EXERCISE 1

A. Underline the subject in each sentence. Follow the example in number 1.

1. <u>Janet</u> works at a bank.
2. Samantha is a dentist.
3. Mrs. Wilkes sits at a desk.
4. He is sending emails.
5. Keiko is a travel agent.
6. They write their customers every week.
7. I am an engineering student.
8. The class and the students are very interesting.

B. Compare answers with another student. Are they the same?

What Is the Verb?

The **verb** tells what the subject *is* or *does*. In a statement (but not in a question), it usually comes after the subject. The verb can be one word or more than one word.

Action Verbs

Many verbs talk about an action. Some examples of action verbs are *work*, *teach*, and *practice*. Look at the underlined action verbs in the examples.

Examples:

Bruce *is working* now.

Mr. Han *teaches* the violin.

They *practice* basketball every day.

Linking Verbs

Some verbs do not show action. They link (connect) the subject to the rest of the sentence. They are called linking verbs. The most common linking verb is *be*. Look at the underlined linking verbs in the examples.

Examples:

Mr. Han *is* a musician.

My aunt and uncle *are* doctors.

EXERCISE 2

A. **Underline the verb in each sentence. Follow the example in number 1.**

1. Janet <u>works</u> at a bank.

2. Mr. and Mrs. Adams own a small business.

3. I am looking for a new job.

4. My friend works part time.

5. We took a short vacation.

6. My new boss speaks English and Spanish.

7. Marsha drinks coffee.

8. The bus is late.

9. They teach Korean in my school.

B. **Compare answers with another student. Are they the same?**

Subject–Verb Agreement

The verb agrees with the subject in an English sentence. That means if the subject is a singular noun or pronoun, the verb is singular. If the subject is a plural noun or pronoun, the verb is plural.

Examples:

Singular Noun / Singular Verb

The barber cuts hair.
The student works hard.
He likes the job.

Plural Noun / Plural Verb

The barbers cut hair.
The students work hard.
They like the job.

EXERCISE 3

A. **Circle the correct verb. Follow the example in number 1.**

1. Amy and Pam (is / are) nurses.
2. Mr. Li (translate / translates) legal documents.
3. My friends (has / have) part-time jobs.
4. My sister (take / takes) pictures at weddings.
5. He (want / wants) his own business.
6. She (make / makes) jewelry.
7. We (serve / serves) food at a restaurant.
8. The Art Institute (give / gives) scholarships every year.

B. **Compare answers with another student. Are they the same?**

EXERCISE 4

Look at the Warm Up on pages 2–3. Correct these groups of words. Make them sentences. Follow the example in number 1.

1. Nick his job. _Nick likes his job._
2. Takes pictures. _____
3. Rachel a photographer. _____
4. Is a salesperson. _____
5. Works hard. _____

Capitalization and Punctuation

When you write sentences in English, follow these guidelines.

Guidelines for Capitalization and End Punctuation

- An English sentence begins with a capital letter (A, B, C, . . .), not a small letter (a, b, c, . . .).

  Example:

  The teacher is busy.

- Most sentences in English end with a period (.). These sentences are called affirmative statements.

  Example:

  I am learning English for my job.

- Use a question mark at the end of sentences that ask a question.

  Examples:

  Are you a student?　　*Where do you work?*　　*How old is your daughter?*

- Use an exclamation point at the end of a sentence to show emotion. We do not use exclamation points very often in English. We save them for when we want to express surprise, anger, or excitement.

  Examples:

  That's a very sad story!　　*You came! I'm surprised!*

Note: In a statement, the verb usually comes after the subject.

*I **am** a student. **I study** every day.*

EXERCISE 5

A. Correct the sentences. Use capital letters and correct punctuation. Follow the example in number 1.

1. he works at the new restaurant

   He works at the new restaurant.

2. what time do you get to work

   _____

(continued)

3. maria likes her job

_____

4. i felt the earthquake in my office

_____

5. jason won the scholarship

_____

6. who is your English teacher

_____

7. that looks fantastic

_____

8. my brother is a journalist

_____

9. do you study Englsh

_____

10. the building is on fire

_____

B. *Compare answers with another student. Are they the same?*

EXERCISE 6

A. *Read the paragraph. Count the number of sentences. How many are there?* _____

    Brian Manning is a travel agent. He owns a small company called Travel with Us. Brian helps people plan their vacations. He helps people plan business trips, too. Brian likes working with people. He enjoys helping them with their travel plans. Brian likes to travel, too. Sometimes he reads about a trip he wants to take. Then he makes his own travel plans. Brian thinks he has the perfect job.

B. *Read the paragraph in Exercise A again. Circle the subject and underline the verb in each sentence.*

C. *Compare answers with another student. Are they the same?*

A. **Work with a partner. Match the subjects to the verb phrases. Follow the example in number 1.**

Subjects		Verb Phrases
1. a doctor	____	**a.** acts in plays or movies
2. an actor	____	**b.** rescues people from burning buildings
3. a chef	____	**c.** prepares food for people
4. a firefighter	____	**d.** writes news articles
5. an architect	_1_	**e.** takes care of sick patients
6. a mechanic	____	**f.** designs buildings and houses
7. a journalist	____	**g.** grows crops and raises animals
8. a farmer	____	**h.** repairs cars and machines

B. **Look at Exercise A again. Write the sentences. Begin each sentence with a capital letter and end it with a period. Follow the example in number 1.**

1. _A doctor takes care of sick patients._____

2. _____

3. _____

4. _____

5. _____

6. _____

7. _____

8. _____

C. **Share your sentences with the class.**

A. *Read the groups of words in the chart. Are they correct sentences? Check (✓) your answers.*

		Yes	No
1.	Yusef works in a hospital.	✓	
2.	My younger brother and sister.		✓
3.	Sells flowers.		
4.	Do you teach Spanish.		
5.	Laura a journalist		
6.	My mother is an architect.		
7.	peter is studying engineering		
8.	I work at a library on campus.		
9.	He delivers the mail.		
10.	Translates from one language to another.		
11.	Started his own business?		
12.	The bank teller cashed my check.		

Remember

A correct sentence has a subject and a verb. It begins with a capital letter and ends with correct punctuation.

B. *Compare answers with another student. Are they the same?*

WORD ORDER IN SENTENCES

In English, the order of words in a sentence is very important. The most common word order for statements is *subject + verb + object* or *complement*.

Subject	Verb	Object / Complement
Pamela	answers	the phone.
Tomoko and Yuki	deliver	mail.
He	does not wear	a uniform.
Pierre	is not	a lawyer.

What Is an Object?

An **object** completes a sentence with more information. The object comes after an action verb. It receives the action. The object can be a noun or a pronoun. It can be one word or more than one word.

Examples:

Subject — Verb — Object (Noun)
The secretary wrote <u>a letter</u>.

Subject — Verb — Object (Pronoun)
She wrote <u>it</u> this morning.

Subject — Verb — Object (Noun)
Flana practices <u>the flute</u> everyday.

Subject — Verb — Object (Noun) — Object (Noun)
She likes <u>jazz</u> and <u>classical music</u>.

What Is a Complement?

A **complement** gives more information about the subject. The complement comes after a linking verb. The complement can be a noun or an adjective.

Examples:

Subject — Linking Verb — Complement (Noun)
Cathy is <u>a lawyer</u>.

Subject — Linking Verb — Complement (Adjective)
She is <u>nice</u>.

Write the words in the correct order to make sentences. Follow the example in number 1.

1. a uniform / she / wears

   She wears a uniform.

2. the waitress / food / serves

   _____

3. three languages / he / speaks

   _____

4. they / in a hotel / work

   _____

5. dangerous / is / her job

   _____

6. takes / Ms. Lee / the bus to work

   _____

7. he / two jobs / has

   _____

8. a tour bus / she / drives

   _____

9. Ali / a new job / wants

   _____

10. is / an editor / Shelley

   _____

USING PERSONAL PRONOUNS AND POSSESSIVE ADJECTIVES

A **pronoun** is a word that can replace a noun in a sentence. The subject and object of a sentence are often a noun. Good writers usually do not repeat the same noun again and again.

There are several kinds of pronouns in English. In this unit, you will learn about **personal pronouns**.

Subject Pronouns

The most common personal pronouns are **subject pronouns**. Subject pronouns often replace noun subjects in sentences. You probably already know and use these pronouns in your writing.

Subject Pronouns	
Singular	**Plural**
I	we
you	you
he, she, it	they

After you write about a specific noun in one sentence, you can replace it with a pronoun in the next sentence. When you use pronouns, you do not have to repeat words. This makes your writing more natural.

Examples:

Less natural: *Antonio is a police officer.* ***Antonio*** *wears a uniform.*
More natural: *Antonio is a police officer.* ***He*** *wears a uniform.*

Less natural: *Antonio and Mark work together.* ***Antonio and Mark*** *are friends.*
More natural: *Antonio and Mark work together.* ***They*** *are friends.*

Less natural: *Mark and I are married.* ***Mark and I*** *have two children.*
More natural: *Mark and I are married.* ***We*** *have two children.*

Complete the sentences. Use the correct subject pronoun. Follow the example in number 1.

1. Dave is very busy. ___He___ takes classes at night, and ___he___ works during the day.

2. My sister designs computer programs. _____ works for a big company.

3. The bus is late again. _____ is always late!

4. Teachers and librarians help people learn. _____ have important jobs.

5. My friend and I are in the same class. _____ study together after school.

6. Mario and Julio are engineers. _____ work for the same company.

Note: A plural pronoun can also replace pronouns.

You and I go to the same school. We can drive to school together.

Object Pronouns

Other personal pronouns are called **object pronouns**. Object pronouns often replace noun objects in sentences.

Object Pronouns	
Singular	**Plural**
me	us
you	you
him, her, it	them

Writers use object pronouns to make their writing more natural.

Examples:

Less natural: _Lisa sells cakes. She bakes **cakes** at home._
More natural: _Lisa sells cakes. She bakes **them** at home._

Less natural: _I bought a cake from Lisa. I served **the cake** for dessert._
More natural: _I bought a cake from Lisa. I served **it** for dessert._

Less natural: _Ms. Kerry is singing. We are listening to **Ms. Kerry**._
More natural: _Ms. Kerry is singing. We are listening to **her**._

A. *Complete the sentences. Write the correct object pronoun for the underlined nouns. Follow the example in number 1.*

1. Mr. Li helped <u>Carl and me</u>. He helped __*us*__ a lot.

2. I bought <u>a new sweater</u>. I'll wear _____ to the party.

3. I did <u>my homework</u>. Then I gave _____ to my teacher.

4. I know <u>Mario</u>. He is my neighbor. I like _____ a lot.

5. <u>Gerry</u> is a great soccer player. I watched _____ play two games yesterday. He made two goals.

6. <u>I</u> can't open the door. Luis forgot to give _____ the keys.

7. <u>Alan</u> missed the bus. _____ was late for class.

8. We took <u>a chemistry exam</u> this morning. _____ was very difficult.

B. *Compare answers with a partner. Are they the same?*

Underline the personal pronouns. Write "S" above the subject pronouns. Write "O" above the object pronouns. Follow the example in number 1.

1. Marsha is a teacher. <u>She</u> teaches French and Spanish.

2. Diego is a doctor. He works in a hospital.

3. I called Rhoda. I asked her to take me to the grocery store.

4. Dennis is a mechanic. He repairs cars.

5. Paul and Bob are business partners. They own a restaurant.

6. Lorraine is angry at her neighbors. She didn't invite them to the dinner party.

7. I live in Edinburgh, Scotland. It has many interesting buildings.

8. Frank can't find his keys. He probably left them at work.

9. Tom and I just got engaged! We are getting married next summer.

A. *Look at the pictures and read the sentences. Write a second sentence for each picture. Use a personal pronoun. Follow the example in number 1.*

1. Barbara is in her office.

   She is talking on the phone.

2. Mr. Marshall is teaching math.

_____

3. Jack and Greg are angry.

_____

4. Pam and Juan are in a restaurant.

_____

5. Stuart is fixing a car.

_____

6. Stephen works for a florist.

_____

B. *Compare sentences with another student. Discuss the ways your sentences are the same or different.*

Possessive Adjectives

Possessive adjectives show that something belongs to someone or something.

Possessive Adjectives	
Singular	**Plural**
my	our
your	your
his, her, its	their

You probably already know these possessive adjectives and use them in many sentences, such as *What's* **your** *name?* **My** *name is Karen.*

Good writers use possessive adjectives to avoid repeating the same nouns. Using possessive adjectives correctly will make your writing more natural.

Examples:

Less natural: *I read Jason's report.* **Jason's** *report was very interesting.*
More natural: *I read Jason's report.* **His** *report was very interesting.*

Less natural: *Carla parks* **Carla's** *car in the garage.*
More natural: *Carla parks* **her** *car in the garage.*

EXERCISE 14

Underline the possessive adjectives.

1. Arnold started his first job last week.

2. Where did Nancy park her car?

3. Evan calls his grandmother once a week.

4. Did you meet our new teacher?

5. They sell their jewelry at a small boutique.

6. I usually do my homework in the library.

7. My roommates do their homework in the library, too.

8. Can I borrow your car? My car is out of gas.

A. *Complete the sentences. Use possessive adjectives. Follow the example in number 1.*

1. Kate's mother is an engineer, and ___*her*___ father is a doctor.

2. I can't call him. I don't know _____ phone number.

3. I just moved. I'll email _____ new address to everyone in the class.

4. Mr. and Mrs. Jones want you to meet _____ grandson.

5. Ann and I finally finished _____ project.

B. *Compare answers with a partner. Are they the same?*

EXERCISE 16

A. *Work with a partner. Take turns. Read the story to your partner.*

Evelyn Field is always busy. Evelyn has two jobs. During the week, Evelyn works at a bank, and on the weekends Evelyn works at a restaurant. Sam is Evelyn's husband. Evelyn and Sam are trying to save enough money to buy a house. Sam doesn't have a job, but Sam works very hard, too. Sam is a medical student. Sam spends a lot of time in classes and studying.

Evelyn and Sam have lots of friends. Evelyn and Sam like to spend time with Evelyn and Sam's friends, but Evelyn is usually too busy. Sam is very busy with school, but Sam has more free time than Evelyn. Sometimes Sam makes plans with Sam's friends. Sam wants Evelyn to quit Evelyn's job at the restaurant. Sam wants to spend more time with Evelyn.

B. *Write the story on a separate piece of paper. Replace the underlined words with subject pronouns, object pronouns, and possessive adjectives.*

C. *Compare stories with another student. Are they the same?*

D. *Work with your class. Read the stories in Exercises A and B aloud. Which story is more natural?*

WRITING TASK

Write sentences about a job.

A. *Prepare for writing. Choose one of these jobs:*

Nurse

Photographer

Firefighter

Carpenter

B. *Write three sentences about the job on a separate piece of paper. (Don't write the name of the job.)*

Examples:

> *He wears a hat.*
>
> *He works in a kitchen.*
>
> *He makes food.*

C. *Work in a group. Take turns. Read your sentences aloud. Other students guess the name of the job.*

Example:

> *He's a chef.*

D. *Give your sentences to the student next to you. Follow these steps:*

1. The person writes one more sentence with a personal pronoun or possessive adjective.

Examples:

> *He wears a hat. His hat is white.*
>
> OR
>
> *He makes food. People like it a lot.*

2. The person passes the sentences to the next person. That person writes a sentence and passes the sentences on.

Examples:

> *He wears a hat. His hat is white. It covers his head.*
>
> OR
>
> *He makes food. People like it a lot. They eat it in his restaurant.*

3. Continue around the group. Take turns. Read the sentences aloud.

4. Play again. Choose another job from the list, or use your own idea.

Check Your Writing

A. *Read your sentences in the Writing Task. Use this form to check your sentences.*

> ### Sentence Checklist
>
> **Each sentence . . .**
>
> - has a subject. ☐
> - has a verb. ☐
> - begins with a capital letter. ☐
> - ends with a period. ☐
> - uses personal pronouns and possessive adjectives correctly. ☐

B. *Correct any errors in your writing. Then write your sentences again.*

> ## Further Practice
>
> ### Journal or Blog Topics
>
> *(See Part 2, Unit 2 and Unit 3, for more information about blogs and journals.)*
>
> - Choose a job from this unit. Write three sentences about the job.
>   ### Example:
>   > *Akemi is an English teacher. She likes her job. She meets interesting people.*
> - Ask a classmate about his or her job. Write three sentences about your classmate and the job.
> - Ask a classmate about his or her classes. Write three sentences about your classmate and his or her classes.
>   ### Example:
>   > *Carlos is a student. He likes his classes. He makes new friends.*

In Part 1, Unit 1, you learned the basic building blocks of sentences in English. In this unit, you will practice adding information to your sentences. This will make your sentences more interesting. Adding more information to your sentences helps your reader "see" into your writing and enjoy your writing more.

You already know that an English sentence has a subject and a verb. Sometimes it has an object or complement.

Example:

Subject   Verb   Object
The woman wrote an email.

You can give more information about the subject (*the woman*) or the object (*an email*). You can add an adjective. The adjective describes the noun.

Example:

Adjective   Adjective
The <u>young</u> woman wrote a <u>funny</u> email.

You can also say more about how the woman wrote the email. You can use an adverb. The adverb describes the verb.

Example:

Adverb
The young woman wrote a funny email <u>quickly</u>.

Warm Up

A.   *Work with a partner. Look at the picture. Talk about what the students are wearing.*

B. **Check the items you see in the picture on page 22.**

☐ jeans ☐ tie ☐ scarf ☐ T-shirt

☐ slacks ☐ jacket ☐ gloves ☐ sweater

☐ dress ☐ coat ☐ shirt ☐ shorts

☐ suit ☐ hat ☐ blouse ☐ skirt

C. **What are you wearing? List four items.**

Examples:

shirt

jeans

_____

_____

_____

_____

D. **Work with another student. What is your partner wearing? List four items.**

_____

_____

_____

_____

E. **Work with the class. Describe your items in Exercises C and D. Make a list of adjectives. Write them on the board.**

Examples:

new shirt

black jeans

Note: Write new words in your vocabulary notebook. *(See Part 4, Unit 1, for more on vocabulary notebooks.)*

USING ADJECTIVES

Good writers add interest to their writing by describing nouns. An **adjective** describes a noun or a pronoun. Adjectives often answer the question *what kind*. For example, adjectives can tell the size, color, age, or quality of something or someone. Adjectives help your reader "see" the person, place, or thing.

Using adjectives in your writing will make it more interesting. Adjectives add details about nouns and help distinguish one noun from other nouns.

Look at the underlined adjectives in the examples.

Examples:

Adjective   Noun

Describing quality: *We ate at an <u>excellent</u> restaurant.*

Adjective Noun

Describing age: *He is watching a <u>new</u> movie.*

Adjective Noun

Describing color: *I bought a <u>red</u> car.*

Pronoun Adjective

Describing size: *It is <u>big</u>.*

Use adjectives correctly when you write. Here are some guidelines.

Guidelines for Using Adjectives

1. An adjective usually comes before the noun it describes.
I like my (sunny) bedroom.

2. An adjective can come after linking verbs such as *be.*
The bedroom is (sunny).

3. Adjectives are always singular. They do not have a plural form.
I love the (beautiful) roses. NOT *I love the beautifuls roses.*

EXERCISE 1

Read the underlined nouns. Circle the adjectives that describe them. Follow the example in number 1.

    1. Miguel's <u>kitchen</u> is (clean).

    2. I like your new <u>shoes</u>.

    3. We put a small <u>table</u> next to the brown <u>sofa</u>.

4. My apartment has high <u>ceilings</u> and large <u>windows</u>.

5. She is wearing a comfortable <u>sweater</u>.

6. Do you like spicy <u>food</u>?

7. This <u>cake</u> is delicious.

8. We moved into an old <u>house</u>.

9. Our <u>neighbors</u> are noisy.

10. Ms. Kahn is an excellent <u>librarian</u>.

EXERCISE 2

A. Read the letter. Circle the adjectives and underline the nouns they describe.

June 14, 2013

Dear Mom and Dad,

I hope you're doing well. Rob and I are spending the weekend in Skaneateles for our anniversary. We are staying at a charming inn called The Arbor. We sent you a postcard. Did you get it? The owner is friendly and helpful. He is also an excellent cook, and he makes us a delicious breakfast every morning. The inn is in a great location. There are nice shops and excellent restaurants close by. The main attraction is the lake. Skaneateles Lake is a beautiful lake. The name Skaneateles means "long lake" in the Iroquois Native American language. On Saturday we rented a boat and went sailing. Later, I bought a terrific painting of the lake. I can't wait for you to see it. Let's all go to Skaneateles for a long weekend together and stay at The Arbor!

Love,

Anna

B. Compare answers with another student.

A. Rewrite the sentences. Add the adjectives in parentheses to describe the underlined nouns. Follow the example in number 1.

1. We have a <u>table</u> in the kitchen. (small)

   We have a small table in the kitchen.

2. I like to relax in my <u>bedroom</u>. (quiet)

   _____

3. The <u>boy</u> ran out of the room. (little)

   _____

4. He likes to drive his <u>car</u>. (new)

   _____

5. We went to some <u>restaurants</u> in Miami. (expensive)

   _____

6. I spent the day reading <u>books</u>. (exciting)

   _____

7. We watched a <u>movie</u> last night. (romantic)

   _____

8. I like to study in <u>places</u>. (comfortable)

   _____

B. Compare answers with another student. Are they the same?

EXERCISE 4

A. Read the sentences. Eight of the sentences have mistakes with adjectives. Correct the eight mistakes. Follow the example in number 1.

1. São Paulo is a city big.

   São Paulo is a big city.

2. She wants a house with three larges bedrooms.

   _____

3. In my hometown, the parks shady are.

_____

4. These sweaters are beautifuls.

_____

5. The chair is comfortable.

_____

6. Canada is a country large.

_____

7. My room is clean.

_____

8. We live in a city safe.

_____

9. My brother little likes trains.

_____

10. I like to study in quiets places.

_____

B. *Compare sentences with another student. Are they the same?*

Combining Sentences with Adjectives

Sometimes you can combine two short sentences into one sentence. Combining sentences is a way to add variety to your writing. Look at the examples.

Examples:

Two sentences about the same hotel: *I work in a hotel. The hotel is busy.*
Combined sentences about the hotel: *I work in a busy hotel.*

Two sentences about the same shirt: *She is wearing a shirt. The shirt is blue.*
Combined sentences about the shirt: *She is wearing a blue shirt.*

The second sentence in each pair of sentences has an adjective. You can move the adjective to the first sentence. This is one way to combine sentences.

A. Combine the sentences. Write new sentences. Follow the example in number 1.

1. My sister lives in a city. The city is big.
   My sister lives in a big city.

2. I tried to cross the street. The street was busy.

3. Junko is wearing a skirt. The skirt is yellow.

4. I like my car. My car is new.

5. I moved to a neighborhood near here. The neighborhood is quiet.

6. The car has seats. The seats are leather.

7. My little brother is wearing a shirt. The shirt is dirty.

8. The Eiffel Tower is a landmark. The landmark is popular.

9. Li works at a hotel. The hotel is elegant.

10. She has a cat. The cat is gray.

B. Compare sentences with a partner. Are they the same?

USING ADVERBS

Good writers also add interest to their sentences by describing verbs. We use **adverbs** to describe verbs. Adverbs often give details about actions. Adverbs will help the reader "see" the action you are describing.

Adverbs that describe action verbs often answer the question *how?* These adverbs usually end in *-ly*. Adverbs usually come after verbs. Look at the underlined adverbs in the examples.

Examples:

          Verb   Adverb
He walked slowly out of the room. (How did he walk? Slowly.)

          Verb   Adverb
She sang beautifully. (How did she sing? Beautifully.)

               Verb Adverb
The teacher spoke softly. (How did the teacher speak? Softly.)

Many times we can make an adverb by adding *-ly* to an adjective.

Adjective	Adverb
nice	nicely
quick	quickly
serious	seriously
easy	easily
careful	carefully
happy	happily
beautiful	beautifully
loud	loudly
smooth	smoothly
angry	angrily

Note: If the adjective ends with the letter *-y*, change *-y* to *-i* and add *-ly* (*easy – easily*).

Some common adverbs have the same form as the adjective.

Adjective	Adverb
fast	fast
high	high
low	low
hard	hard
late	late

Note: *Good* has an irregular adverb form. The adverb form is *well.*

EXERCISE 6

Read the underlined verbs. Circle the adverbs that describe them.

1. Nancy <u>entered</u> the house (quietly).
2. She <u>waved</u> good-bye happily.
3. My brother <u>snores</u> loudly.
4. She <u>waited</u> patiently for the doctor.
5. My father <u>yelled</u> angrily.
6. Nadia <u>wrote</u> her name neatly.
7. The fire <u>spread</u> quickly.
8. Steve <u>answered</u> the question easily.
9. I <u>drove</u> carefully down the dark street.
10. Please <u>watch</u> the children closely.

EXERCISE 7

A. *Correct the adverb mistake in each sentence. Follow the example in number 1.*

1. You should talk ~~quiet~~ *quietly* in the library.
2. Yoko drives careful.
3. Felix came to school lately today.

4. My teacher speaks soft. I can't understand him.

5. My friend plays the piano very beautiful.

6. We ran home very fastly after school.

7. He yelled angry at the dog.

8. The team played very good.

B. *Compare answers with another student. Are they the same?*

EXERCISE 8

A. *Write the answers. Use the adverbs from the box. Adverbs may be used more than once. Follow the example in number 1.*

beautifully	fast	loudly	seriously
carefully	happily	noisily	slowly
easily	hard	quickly	softly

1. How do you work?

   I work hard.

2. How do you drive?

3. How do you speak?

4. How does your favorite musician sing?

5. How do you walk?

6. How do you work in school?

7. How do soccer fans usually cheer?

B. *Compare answers with another student. Are they the same?*

USING PREPOSITIONAL PHRASES

You just practiced making your sentences more interesting by adding details with adjectives and adverbs. You can also use prepositional phrases to add variety and interest to your writing.

What Is a Phrase?

A **phrase** is a small group of words. Together, they have a particular meaning. There are many kinds of phrases in English. In this unit, you will practice using prepositional phrases.

What Is a Prepositional Phrase?

A **prepositional phrase** is a phrase that begins with a preposition and includes a noun or a pronoun. Prepositions are words like *in, on,* and *at.* Prepositional phrases often answer the question *where.* These phrases are called *prepositional phrases of place.* Other prepositional phrases answer the question *when.* These phrases are called *prepositional phrases of time.*

Examples:

Prepositional phrase
She put the book <u>on the desk</u>. (prepositional phrase of place)

Prepositional phrase
I'll meet you <u>at noon</u>. (prepositional phrase of time)

EXERCISE 9

A. *Underline the prepositional phrase in each sentence. Then circle "Place" or "Time."*

1. I saw Marco <u>at the library</u>.　　　　(Place)　Time
2. The meeting starts in an hour.　　　Place　Time
3. I live on Short Street.　　　　　　　Place　Time
4. It usually rains here in the summer.　Place　Time
5. Henry has a dentist appointment on Tuesday.　Place　Time
6. The university is in Paris.　　　　　Place　Time
7. We are going on vacation in June.　Place　Time
8. I went to sleep at midnight.　　　　Place　Time

B. *Compare answers with another student. Are they the same?*

Prepositional Phrases with *In*, *At*, and *On*

Three of the most common prepositions in English are *in*, *at*, and *on*. We often use these prepositions in phrases about time and place.

Time		
In	**At**	**On**
Use "in" for months and years: • *in March* • *in 2012* Use "in" for a period of time in the future: • *in a few months* • *in a couple of weeks* Use "in" for seasons: • *in the spring* • *in the winter* Use "in" for a part of the day: • *in the morning* • *in the afternoon* • *in the evening* • (but <u>*at night*</u>)	Use "at" with an exact time: • *at three o'clock* • *at 9:45* • *at 2:00 P.M.* • *at noon* • *at midnight*	Use "on" with days of the week: • *on Wednesday* • *on Fridays* Use "on" with dates and holidays: • *on February 3, 2014* • *on February 3* • *on Thanksgiving*

Place		
In	**At**	**On**
Use "in" with countries, states, and cities: • *in Japan* • *in Colorado* • *in Seoul* Use "in" with enclosed spaces: • *in my bedroom* • *in the library* • *in the office*	Use "at" with addresses and specific places: • *at 1605 North Elm Street* • *at the train station* • *at the theater*	Use "on" with names of streets, roads, boulevards, and avenues: • *on Spruce Street* • *on Eastern Road*

Complete the sentences. Use "in," "on," or "at."

1. I have an important meeting _____ 8:00 A.M.
2. The store is closed _____ August.
3. Do you work _____ Fridays?
4. Her birthday is _____ July 16.
5. I usually take a nap _____ the afternoon.
6. In Vermont, it often snows _____ December.
7. The restaurant closes _____ midnight.
8. Where will you be _____ New Year's Day?
9. She was born _____ 1998.
10. What time do you get up _____ the morning?

EXERCISE 11

A. *Answer the questions. Write complete sentences with "in," "on," or "at."*

1. What time does your class start?

   _____

2. When is Valentine's Day?

   _____

3. When do you usually go on vacation?

   _____

4. When do you eat breakfast?

   _____

5. When do you celebrate your birthday?

   _____

6. What time do the stores usually close in your hometown?

   _____

B. *Share answers with another student.*

Complete the conversations with "in," "on," or "at."

1. **Cathy:** Guess what? I'm moving to your neighborhood. What's the name of your street?

   Lana: I live _____ West Avenue.

   Cathy: Great. I'll be right around the corner _____ East Street. Doesn't Luis live _____ West Avenue, too?

   Lana: Yes. He's _____ 35 West Avenue. I'm _____ 47 West Avenue. It's just a few houses away.

   Cathy: That's wonderful. We'll all be neighbors!

2. **Gail:** I just got an email from John. He's _____ Japan for six months.

   Dave: Really! What's he doing there?

   Gail: He's teaching English _____ a small language school _____ Tokyo.

   Dave: That sounds great! Let's go visit him!

   Gail: Count me in!

Prepositional Phrases with Places

We often use prepositional phrases to describe places. You learned about the prepositions *at, in,* and *on.* We use them to tell where things are located. English has many other prepositions we use in phrases to tell the position of things.

Study the chart of other common prepositions we use to write about places.

Prepositions of Place	
above	across (from)
behind	between
in back of	in front of
near	next to
on top of	under

EXERCISE 13

Underline the prepositional phrase in each sentence. Follow the example in number 1.

1. A new bank opened <u>next to the library</u>.
2. The cat is hiding behind the chair.
3. He left his keys on top of the dresser.
4. My shoes are under the bed.
5. There is a small table between the beds.
6. We planted several trees in front of the house.
7. The painting is above the fireplace.
8. We had a picnic near the lake.
9. My best friend lives across the street.

EXERCISE 14

Read the paragraph. Underline the prepositional phrases.

My university is small, but it has a beautiful campus. The campus is <u>next to a small lake.</u> There are comfortable benches and chairs near the lake. I like to sit on a bench and watch the ducks in the water. There is also a large grassy area in front of the library. There are many buildings on campus, but my favorite is the castle. It is behind the main entrance. Best of all, there are magnificent trees next to every path.

EXERCISE 15

A. *Read the note on the next page. Use the picture to help you complete the sentences. Use the prepositional phrases from the box.*

above the fireplace	next to the sofa
between the chairs	~~on the coffee table~~
in the bookcase	on the sofa
next to the lamp	on top of the bookcase

Hi Cathy,

Susan is coming home tonight. We need to get the apartment ready before she gets here. I cleaned the bathroom and kitchen. Can you clean the living room? Here is a list of the things you need to do. The candy and fruit are on the kitchen table.

Thanks!

Liz

1. Buy some flowers and put them in the vase _____on the coffee table_____.
2. Put the "Welcome Home Susan" sign on the wall _____.
3. Put the books _____.
4. Put the pillows _____.
5. Put the magazines on the small table _____.
6. Put the candy in the bowl _____.
7. Put the fruit in the basket _____.
8. Empty the trash and put the trash can _____.

B. Compare answers with another student. Are they the same?

There is and *There are*

You practiced using prepositional phrases to describe where things are located.

We can also tell the location of things with the phrases ***there is*** or ***there are***. Look at the example. These two sentences have the same meaning, but the second sentence is more common.

Examples:

> *A magazine is on the table.*
> ***There is** a magazine on the table.*

We use ***there is*** to talk about one thing and ***there are*** to talk about two or more things.

Sentences that begin with *there is* or *there are* have a special word order. In most English sentences, the subject comes before the verb. But when you begin a sentence with *there is* or *there are,* the subject comes after the verb (*is* or *are*). Additional information about the subject comes after the subject. The additional information is often about a place.

Look at the example sentences.

Examples:

> Subject Additional information
> *There is a plant on the table.* (Where is the plant? It is on the table.)

> Subject Additional information
> *There are some pencils in the drawer.* (Where are the pencils? They are in the drawer.)

> Subject Additional information
> *There is a map of Africa on the wall.* (Where is the map? It is on the wall.)

When the subject is singular, you use ***there is***. When the subject is plural, you use ***there are***. Sometimes it is difficult to decide whether to use *there is* or *there are*. The first thing you need to do is identify the subject.

> **Note:** The word ***there*** is NOT the subject of the sentence.

Examples:

> Subject
> *There is a car in the driveway.* (The subject *car* is singular, so we use the singular verb *is*.)

> Subject
> *There are several cars in the driveway.* (The subject *cars* is plural, so we use the plural verb *are*.)

Complete each sentence with "There is" or "There are."

1. <u>There are</u> many photographs of my family on the wall.

2. _____ an interesting painting above the fireplace.

3. _____ several apples in the bowl.

4. _____ a lamp next to the table.

5. _____ a new rug on the floor in the living room.

6. _____ two comfortable blue chairs in front of the TV.

7. _____ several maps on the wall above the sofa.

8. _____ a small bookcase near the door.

Read the sentences. Seven of the sentences have mistakes in the verb. Correct the verbs. Follow the example in number 1.

1. There ~~are~~ *is* a dictionary on the desk.

2. There is several magazines on the table.

3. There is a mirror on the wall.

4. There are a comfortable chair in the hall.

5. There are a blue pillow on the bed.

6. There is three windows in my bedroom.

7. There are several new students in the class.

8. There are a ruler in the drawer.

9. There is many fish in the fish tank.

10. There are lots of interesting pieces of art in this room.

A. *Work with another student. Look around your classroom. Write sentences about your classroom. Begin each sentence with "There is" or "There are."*

1. _____

2. _____

3. _____

4. _____

5. _____

B. *Join another pair. Compare sentences.*

WRITING TASK

Write a short description.

A. *Prepare for writing. Follow these steps:*

1. Choose one of these topics:
   - Your favorite clothing
   - Your favorite room in your house
   - Your favorite sport or your favorite team
   - Your favorite musician or band
   - A city you love
   - Something you like to do
   - A place at your school

2. Make a list of adjectives, adverbs, and prepositional phrases to describe your topic.

B. *Write six sentences about the topic on a separate piece of paper. Use the adjectives, adverbs, and prepositional phrases from your list. Use "there is" or "there are" in at least one sentence.*

C. *Work in a group. Take turns. Read your sentences aloud.*

Check Your Writing

A. *Read your sentences in the Writing Task. Use this form to check your sentences.*

Sentence Checklist

Each sentence . . .

- has a subject. ☐
- has a verb. ☐
- begins with a capital letter. ☐
- ends with a period. ☐
- uses at least one of these correctly: an adjective, an adverb, ☐
  a prepositional phrase, *there is* or *there are*.

B. *Correct any errors in your sentences. Then write your sentences again.*

Further Practice

Journal or Blog Topic

(See Part 2, Unit 2 and Unit 3, for more information about blogs and journals.)

- Look in a magazine, a comic book, or online. Find a picture of a real person, a superhero, or a cartoon character.
  - Write five sentences about the person or cartoon character.
  - Describe the clothes.
  - Use adjectives.
  - Include a picture if possible.

Simple and Compound Sentences

There are several kinds of sentences in English. In Part 1, Unit 1, you learned that a sentence is a group of words with a subject and a verb. A sentence with one subject and one verb is a **simple sentence**.

In this unit, you will continue writing simple sentences. You will also combine simple sentences to form **compound sentences**. Good writers vary their sentences. They use both simple and compound sentences in their writing. A variety of sentences makes the writing more interesting for the reader.

Warm Up

A. *Work in a group. Look at the picture. Discuss these questions:*

- What is Don doing?
- What is Helen doing?
- What kind of movie do you think they are watching? Why?

Don and Helen are watching a movie on TV.

B. *Look at the list of kinds of movies. Check (✓) the three kinds you like the most. Then write the name of a movie you like for each kind that you checked.*

☐ Comedies _____

☐ Science fiction _____

☐ Thrillers _____

☐ Romance _____

☐ Westerns _____

☐ Action _____

☐ Adventure _____

☐ Dramas _____

☐ Musicals _____

☐ Fantasy _____

☐ Mystery _____

☐ Crime _____

☐ Animated _____

C. *Compare your list with another student. Do you like the same kinds of movies? Do you like the same movies?*

D. *Write five sentences. Write about your list and your classmate's list in Exercise C.*

Examples:

> *I like fantasy movies.*
> *My favorite fantasy movie is* Ghostbusters.
> *Maria doesn't like fantasy movies.*
> *She likes musicals.*
> *Her favorite musical is* Mama Mia.

1. _____

2. _____

3. _____

4. _____

5. _____

SIMPLE SENTENCES

Simple sentences are the most basic type of sentence. They are often very short. A simple sentence usually has one subject and one verb.

Subject Verb
Helen likes funny movies.

A simple sentence can also have more than one subject.

Subject   Subject
Helen and Don like funny movies.

It can have more than one verb.

Verb   Verb
Don is watching a movie and eating popcorn.

The Simple Sentence: Two Subjects

Most simple sentences have one subject. But some simple sentences have two subjects. The subjects are connected with *and*. When you write a sentence with two subjects, make sure the verb is plural.

Examples:

Sylvia likes romance movies. (There is one subject and the verb is singular: *likes*)
Donna likes romance movies. (There is one subject and the verb is singular: *likes*)
Sylvia and Donna like romance movies. (There are two subjects and the verb is plural: *like*)

Grown Ups is a funny movie. (There is one subject and the verb is singular: *is*)
Home Alone is a funny movie. (There is one subject and the verb is singular: *is*)
Grown Ups and Home Alone are funny movies. (There are two subjects and the verb is plural: *are*)

A. *Underline the two subjects in each sentence. Circle the verb. Follow the example in number 1.*

1. <u>My brother</u> and <u>I</u> (like) science fiction movies.
2. Soccer and tennis are my favorite sports.
3. Her mother and father go to the movies every weekend.
4. Janice and Catherine play lacrosse.
5. Coins and stamps are fun to collect.
6. Alex and Joanna run everyday.
7. Sharif and his father like soccer.
8. Whales and dolphins are mammals.
9. My sister and brother are twins.
10. Henry and I work together.

B. *Compare answers with another student. Are they the same?*

A. *Circle the correct verb in each sentence.*

1. My sister and I (collect / collects) dolls from around the world.
2. My mother and my aunt (give / gives) knitting classes.
3. Monica (enjoy / enjoys) going to parties.
4. Pedro and Juan (play / plays) basketball on the weekend.
5. Her younger brother (is / are) the captain of the soccer team.
6. I (like / likes) Westerns a lot.
7. Sharks and turtles (swim / swims) in the ocean.
8. Marisol (enjoy / enjoys) cooking.
9. My mother (prefer / prefers) comedies, but my father (enjoy / enjoys) mysteries.
10. Nancy and her husband (is / are) musicians.

B. *Compare answers with another student. Are they the same?*

Work with another student. Read the information in the chart. Make guesses and complete the sentences about Carla, Derek, and Amanda. Follow the example in number 1.

	Carla	**Derek**	**Amanda**
Hobbies	Photography Reading	Reading Gardening	Gardening Photography
Favorite Sports	Tennis Soccer	Soccer Baseball	Tennis Baseball
Favorite Movie Types	Action Romance	Action Thriller	Romance Thriller

1. _____*Derek*_____ and _____*Amanda*_____ like gardening.

2. _____ and _____ play tennis.

3. _____ and _____ watch action movies.

4. _____ and _____ like photography.

5. _____ and _____ play baseball.

6. _____ and _____ watch romance movies.

7. _____ and _____ like reading.

8. _____ and _____ play soccer.

9. _____ and _____ watch thrillers.

Combine the sentences. Follow the example in number 1.

1. Alejandro plays soccer every Saturday. Erik plays soccer every Saturday.

   Alejandro and Erik play soccer every Saturday.

2. Running is good exercise. Riding a bike is good exercise.

   _____

3. Jane joined the volleyball team. Stacy joined the volleyball team.

   _____

4. Gardening is a fun hobby. Photography is a fun hobby.

   _____

5. Mountain climbing is dangerous. Extreme skiing is dangerous.

   _____

6. Shira reads mysteries. Jaimie reads mysteries.

   _____

7. Rosalind collects dolls. Her sister collects dolls.

   _____

8. Hockey is a team sport. Baseball is a team sport.

   _____

9. Erin likes to shop. Serena likes to shop.

   _____

10. Jackson watches movies on TV. Austin watches movies on TV.

    _____

Remember

When you write a sentence with two subjects joined by *and*, make sure the verb is plural.

A. *Work with your class. Find two classmates with the same hobby. Write their names in the chart.*

Example:

> **Student 1:** *What's your hobby?*
>
> **Student 2:** *I like gardening.* OR *My hobby is gardening.* OR *I garden.*

Hobbies	Student 1	Student 2
taking photographs		
gardening		
reading		
watching movies		
playing tennis		
playing soccer		
fishing		
dancing		
playing golf		
doing arts and crafts		
playing a musical instrument		
watching TV		
shopping		
other:		

B. *Work in a small group. Use the chart in Exercise A. Write sentences about your classmates. Use "and" to connect the two subjects.*
Example:

Abdul and Hamid like gardening.

1. _____
2. _____
3. _____
4. _____
5. _____

Remember
Use a capital letter at the beginning of each sentence and a period at the end.

C. *Share your sentences with another group.*

The Simple Sentence: Two Verbs

Most simple sentences have one verb. But some simple sentences have two verbs. The verbs are connected with *and*.

Examples:

Mandy reads books. (There is one subject and one verb: *reads*)
Mandy writes books. (There is one subject and one verb: *writes*)
Mandy reads and writes books. (There is one subject and two verbs: *reads* and *writes*)

Some simple sentences have two subjects and two verbs. Connect the subjects with *and*. Then connect the verbs with *and*. Remember: When you write a sentence with two subjects joined by *and*, make sure the verbs are plural.

Examples:

Mandy and Karen read books. (There are two subjects and one verb. The verb is plural: *read*)
Mandy and Karen write books. (There are two subjects and one verb. The verb is plural: *write*)
Mandy and Karen read and write books. (There are two subjects and two verbs. The verbs are plural: *read* and *write*)

Underline the subjects. Double underline the verbs. Circle the word "and."
Follow the example in number 1.

1. Emma (and) Jonathan write (and) sing songs at night.
2. Keiko plays and watches ping-pong on Saturdays.
3. Benjamin and his brother collect and sell coins.
4. Eleanor paints and photographs beautiful flowers.
5. Sandra washes and irons her shirts on the weekend.
6. My friends and I write and perform plays at school.

EXERCISE 7

Combine the sentences. Follow the example in number 1.

1. Joe reads poetry. Joe writes poetry.

   Joe reads and writes poetry.

2. Abdul rents movies on Saturdays. Abdul watches movies on Saturdays.

   _____

3. My roommate finds new recipes. My roommate tries new recipes.

   _____

4. I hike in the summer. I go camping in the summer.

   _____

5. My friend and I swim in the lake next to my house. My friend and I go fishing in the lake next to my house.

   _____

6. The store sells computers. The store repairs computers.

   _____

Remember

Connect the two verbs with *and*. Do not repeat the words that are the same in both sentences.

COMPOUND SENTENCES

Good writers use different kinds of sentences in their writing. They write short simple sentences. They also write longer sentences. This sentence variety is important for good writing.

So far, you have practiced writing short, simple sentences. Now you will learn about joining sentences into longer, **compound sentences**. Use both kinds of sentences in your writing.

What Is a Compound Sentence?

We make compound sentences by joining two simple sentences with a connecting word. The most common connecting words are *and*, *but*, and *so*.

> **Examples:**
>
> *Josh likes soccer.* (simple sentence)
> *He plays every afternoon.* (simple sentence)
> *Josh likes soccer, **and** he plays every afternoon.* (compound sentence)
>
> *Isabelle likes rock music.* (simple sentence)
> *She doesn't like jazz.* (simple sentence)
> *Isabelle likes rock music, **but** she doesn't like jazz.* (compound sentence)
>
> *Yumi likes to cook.* (simple sentence)
> *She usually makes dinner.* (simple sentence)
> *Yumi likes to cook, **so** she usually makes dinner.* (compound sentence)

Compound sentences always have a comma (**,**) and a connecting word. Put the comma before the connecting word.

Using *And* in Compound Sentences

We use **and** to join two simple sentences that have similar ideas. The second sentence adds information to the first sentence.

The two subjects in many compound sentences are the same.

> **Example:**
>
> *Jack reads history books, **and** he watches a history channel on TV.*

The two subjects in some compound sentences are different, but the ideas are related.

> **Example:**
>
> *I collect comic books, **and** my brother collects baseball cards.*

Read the compound sentences. Circle the subjects. Underline the verbs. Double underline the connecting word. Follow the example in number 1.

1. (Hockey) is an exciting game, and (fans) love it.
2. Kim paints pictures, and her husband sells them.
3. The boys played on one team, and the girls played on the other team.
4. The teacher is talking, and the students are listening.
5. I am listening to music, and my roommate is watching TV.
6. Nathan builds the bookcases, and Harrison paints them.

Remember

Compound sentences always have a comma (,) before the connecting word *and*.

Combine the sentences with "and." Follow the example in number 1.

1. Min Ho is tired. He wants to go home.

   Min Ho is tired, and he wants to go home.

2. The sun is shining. The sky is blue.

   _____

3. Ann made dinner. Larry set the table.

   _____

4. Kayo writes letters. Her parents write emails.

   _____

5. It rained on Monday. It snowed on Tuesday.

   _____

6. Jason bought a new camera. He uses it every day.

   _____

7. I go to school in the morning. I work in the afternoon.

_____

8. The days are warm. The nights are mild.

_____

Using *But* in Compound Sentences

We use *but* to join two simple sentences that have different opposite ideas. *But* shows a contrast between the two simple sentences. The compound sentence can talk about the same subject in both parts of the sentence, or different subjects.

Examples:

I love to travel, **but** *I hate to fly.*

I like outdoor activities, **but** *my husband likes indoor activities.*

EXERCISE 10

Read the compound sentences. Circle the subjects. Underline the verbs. Double underline the connecting word. Follow the example in number 1.

1. Nadia wants to go to the movies, but she has to study.

2. I enjoy gardening, but I don't like to cut the lawn.

3. I like comedies, but I don't like thrillers.

4. We like to exercise, but we don't like the gym.

5. Paul loves summertime, but Sarah doesn't like the heat.

6. Yun wants to study, but her roommate wants to play loud music.

7. Akiko wants to take piano lessons, but she doesn't have time.

8. My family is small, but my husband's family is big.

A. *Match a simple sentence in Column A with a contrasting simple sentence in Column B.*

A	B
1. Sanah wants to go to the movies.	____ **a.** Bill wants to go to a late show.
2. Sanah likes romance movies.	____ **b.** Bill likes to drive.
3. Sanah wants to go to an early show.	_1_ **c.** Bill wants to watch TV.
4. Sanah likes to walk to the theater.	____ **d.** Bill wants to go to a restaurant.
5. Sanah wants to eat at home.	____ **e.** Bill wants to sit in the back of the theater.
6. Sanah wants to sit near the front of the theater.	____ **f.** Bill likes thrillers.

Remember

Compound sentences always have a comma (,) before the connecting word *but*.

B. *Combine the sentences in Exercise A with "but." Follow the example in number 1.*

1. *Sanah wants to go to the movies, but Bill wants to watch TV.*

2. _____

3. _____

4. _____

5. _____

6. _____

C. *Compare sentences with a partner. Are they the same?*

Using *So* in Compound Sentences

We use **so** to connect a simple sentence that gives a result (or cause) with a simple sentence that tells the reason (or cause). When you write a compound sentence with **so**, put the reason (or cause) at the beginning of the sentence. The compound sentence can have the same or a different subject in the two parts of the sentence.

Examples:

Reason   Result

Henry has two jobs, **so** *he doesn't have a lot of free time.*

- The reason in the first part is *has two jobs.*
- The result of having two jobs is *doesn't have a lot of free time.*

Reason   Result

Carl and Janet love this movie, **so** *they saw it again last night.*

- The reason in the first part is *love this movie.*
- The result of loving this movie is *saw it again.*

EXERCISE 12

A. **Read the compound sentences. Circle the subjects. Underline the verbs. Double underline the connecting word. Follow the example in number 1.**

1. (It) is raining, so (you) can't go swimming now.

2. I want to dance well, so I am taking dance lessons.

3. Ilhan has a broken leg, so he can't go skiing.

4. I love flowers, so my friend gave me flowers for my birthday.

5. We are late, so we have to hurry.

6. I have some free time, so you can come and visit now.

7. She did a great job on the project, so she got a promotion at work.

8. Astrid missed the bus, so she was late for class.

9. I can't see the blackboard, so I moved my seat to the front of the classroom.

10. He wants to study in the United States, so he is learning English.

B. **Compare answers with a partner. Are they the same?**

EXERCISE 13

A. Match the reasons to the results.

The Reason	The Result
1. It's a beautiful day.	____ **a.** He rests on the weekend.
2. It's a stormy day.	____ **b.** You need a coat.
3. I like team sports.	____ **c.** I joined a baseball team.
4. It's cold tonight.	_1_ **d.** We can have a picnic.
5. He works hard all week.	____ **e.** They can't play outside.

Remember

Compound sentences always have a comma (,) before the connecting word *so.*

B. Combine the sentences in Exercise A with "so." Follow the example in item 1.

1. _It's a beautiful day, so we can have a picnic._
2. _____
3. _____
4. _____
5. _____

C. Compare sentences with a partner. Are they the same?

EXERCISE 14

Combine the simple sentences into one compound sentence. Use the connecting word in parentheses. Follow the example in number 1.

1. I enjoy watching basketball on TV. I don't like playing it. (but)

   I enjoy watching basketball on TV, but I don't like playing it.

2. Hockey is popular in Canada. Many famous hockey players are Canadian. (and)

   _____

3. Sharon likes winter sports. Her boyfriend prefers summer sports. (but)

   _____

4. I want a new guitar. I'm saving my money. (so)

_____

5. Hassan plays backgammon with his friends. He plays chess with his father. (and)

_____

6. I like volleyball. I'm not very good at it. (but)

_____

7. He doesn't like mysteries. He hates romance novels. (and)

_____

8. Paula likes making things to wear. Knitting is a good hobby for her. (so)

_____

EXERCISE 15

Combine the simple sentences into one compound sentence. Use "and," "but," or "so."

1. My computer is broken. I can't check my email.

My computer is broken, so I can't check my email.

2. Winston teaches guitar. He plays in a band.

_____

3. Luis is interested in old money. He started a coin collection.

_____

4. Sue and Ed like snow skiing in the winter. They like waterskiing in the summer.

_____

5. Tom likes cooking. He hates doing the dishes.

_____

6. I like to go to the mall. I like to shop online.

_____

7. My car doesn't work. I take the bus.

_____

A. *Work with another student. Discuss the hobbies in the chart.*

- Which words describe your feelings about the hobby?
- Check (✓) the descriptions that are true for you.

Hobbies	Descriptions							
	fun	boring	easy	difficult	safe	dangerous	relaxing	stressful
swimming								
reading								
mountain climbing								
hiking								
surfing								
watching TV								
other (your own idea): _____								

B. *Write the beginning of a compound sentence on a separate piece of paper. Use information from the chart.*

- Work with a partner. Exchange the beginning of your sentences.
- Complete the compound sentence.
- Take turns writing and completing your partner's sentences.

Examples:

Student A writes: *Swimming is easy, but*

Student B writes: *Swimming is easy, but surfing is difficult.*

Student B writes: *Watching TV is boring, so*

Student A writes: *Watching TV is boring, so I don't watch a lot of TV.*

WRITING TASK

Write about hobbies.

A. **Prepare for writing. Read the information in your class survey on page 48.**

B. **Write four simple sentences about your classmates' hobbies. Use "and" to combine subjects and verbs.**
   Examples:
   Carlos and I like action movies.
   Mary gardens and plays tennis.

   1. _____
   2. _____
   3. _____
   4. _____

C. **Write four compound sentences about your classmates' hobbies. Use "and," "but," and "so" to combine sentences.**
   Examples:
   Abdul plays tennis, but he doesn't play soccer.
   Keiko likes romance movies, and Yumi likes action movies.
   Marcella loves science fiction movies, so she always goes to see them.

   1. _____
   2. _____
   3. _____
   4. _____

D. **Work in a group. Take turns. Read your sentences in Exercises B and C aloud.**

Check Your Writing

A. *Read your sentences in the Writing Task. Use this form to check your sentences.*

> ### Sentence Checklist
>
> **Each sentence . . .**
>
> - has the correct subjects and verbs. ☐
> - has a connecting word. ☐
> - has a comma before the connecting word. ☐
> - begins with a capital letter. ☐
> - ends with a period. ☐

B. *Correct any errors in your sentences. Then write your sentences again.*

Further Practice

Play a game with your group. Follow these steps:

1. Use a separate piece of paper. Write three compound sentences about your hobbies or activities. Use *and* in one sentence, *but* in another sentence, and *so* in the third sentence.
2. Work in a group. Put all the papers together. Mix them up and put them in a pile.
3. Take turns. Pick a paper and read the sentences aloud.
4. Who wrote the sentences? Guess the name of the student.

Social and Personal Writing

Friendly Letters and Postcards

People write for many different reasons, and there are many different kinds of writing. Some kinds of writing are more formal. For example, writing for school or work is more formal writing. Some kinds of writing are not very formal, for example, writing for yourself or writing to friends or family is less formal. In this unit, you will practice some less formal kinds of social writing.

What Is Social Writing?

- Writing to friends and family members
- Writing friendly letters, postcards, emails, text messages
- Writing blogs and newsletters
- Writing in an informal way

Why Is Social Writing Important?

Social writing is a good way to communicate with your friends and family. You can write to them often. You can share information with them. This will help you become better at expressing your ideas in writing. Social writing is a fun way to practice writing.

Warm Up

A. *Look at the pictures. What do you think each person is doing? Match the pictures with the correct phrases. Complete the sentences on the next page.*

| writing a letter | writing a postcard | writing an email |

a

b

c

a. This person is _____.

b. This person is _____.

c. This person is _____.

B. **Work with another student. Discuss these questions:**

- Do you write letters to friends or family members? Who do you write to?
- When do you write?
- How often do you receive letters from friends or family members?
- Do you usually send postcards when you are traveling?
- Do you like to receive letters and postcards from friends?

SOCIAL

FRIENDLY LETTERS

Friendly letters are also called *personal* letters or *informal* letters. You usually use informal or casual language in friendly letters. That means you write the same way that you speak to your friend or family member. People write friendly letters for many reasons. Think about the reasons you write friendly letters.

A. **Look at the reasons people write friendly letters. Check (✓) the reasons that are true for you. Add two more reasons.**

☐ send news about yourself

☐ make plans together

☐ tell about a book you read

☐ ask for advice

☐ congratulate someone on a new job

☐ _____

☐ _____

B. **Compare your answers with another student. Are they the same?**

The Parts of a Letter

Friendly letters usually have five parts: the **heading, greeting, body, closing,** and **signature**. Read the information about the five parts.

Heading

The heading always includes the date. You can also include your address.

- If you only want to include the date, write it on the first line, in the upper right corner.
- If you include your address, write your street address on the first line. Write your city, state, and zip code on the next line. Write the date on the third line.

Note: You usually do not need to include your address in a friendly letter. You can write only the date.

Greeting

The second part of the letter is the greeting. The greeting begins with a capital letter (for example, *D* or *H)* and ends with a comma (,) after the person's name. Leave one line between the heading and the greeting.

The most common greeting for friendly letters is:

    Dear _____ *,*

Other greetings you can use are:

    Hi, _____ *,*   *Hello,* _____ *,*

Body

The body of the letter is the third part. It is the message you write. Leave one line between the greeting and the body.

Closing

The closing is a polite way to end your letter. The closing usually lines up with the heading. Begin the closing with a capital letter and end it with a comma (,).

Some common closings are:

    Love,   *Your friend,*   *Take care,*

Signature

The signature is your name. Write your name under the closing.

A. Work with another student. Label the parts of the letter.

<u>heading</u> ⎡ 55 Dover Street
Exton, PA 10102
⎣ March 19, 2013

Dear Sarah, ⎤

   How are you? I'm sorry I didn't write sooner. I moved into a new apartment last week. I'm living with my sister Ana. We have an apartment near campus. It's small, but it's nice.

   School started last week. My classes are interesting. I made a good friend in my English class. Her name is Claudia. She's from Brazil, and she speaks Portuguese. She's studying English. Claudia's very friendly and nice. She likes to play tennis. We played a game together, and she beat me! Claudia also loves to travel. We're planning to go to New York City next weekend. We're going to stay with her aunt and uncle.

   I hope you can come visit me soon. I want you to see my new apartment and meet Claudia. You will like her a lot. Ana sends her love. Please write soon.

⎡ Love,
⎣ Becky

SOCIAL

B. Read the letter again. Work with a partner. Answer the questions.

1. Who wrote the letter? Circle the answer.
   a. Becky   **b.** Sarah   **c.** Claudia

2. Who received the letter? Circle the answer.
   a. Ana   **b.** Sarah   **c.** Becky

(continued)

3. When was the letter written? _____

4. Who are Sarah and Becky? Circle the answer.

    a. sisters

    b. friends

    c. co-workers

5. What is the letter about? Circle the answer.

    a. an invitation

    b. learning English

    c. news about the writer

6. Where does Becky live? _____

EXERCISE 2

A. *Discuss these questions with a partner. Write your partner's answers on the lines. Write complete sentences.*

1. What is your name?

_____

2. Where are you from?

_____

3. What language(s) do you speak?

_____

4. Why are you learning English?

_____

5. What else are you studying?

_____

6. Do you have a job? Where do you work?

_____

7. What do you do in your free time?

_____

B. *Complete a letter to a friend or family member. Write about your partner. Use the answers in Exercise A and the correct word in parentheses in the letter. Remember to include a heading, greeting, closing, and your signature.*

✳ ✳ ✳ ✳

SOCIAL

_____
_____
_____

Dear _____,

    How are you? I'm fine. School is going well. I made a new friend in my English class. _____ name is _____.
                 (His / Her)
_____ is from _____. _____
  (He / She)   (He / She)
speaks _____. _____ is learning English
                  (He / She)
because _____. _____ is also
                          (He / She)
studying _____. _____ _____
              (He / She)   (has / doesn't have)
a job. In _____ free time, _____ likes to
        (his / her)   (name)
_____. I hope you can meet my new

friend soon.

                        _____
                        _____

C. **Read the letter your partner wrote about you. Discuss these questions:**

1. Is the information about you correct? If not, correct the information.

2. Did your partner include all of the parts of a friendly letter? If not, help your partner correct the letter.

Capitalization and Punctuation Rules for Letters

There are many rules for capitalization and punctuation in English. Look at the rules on the next page for correct capitalization and punctuation in friendly letters.

Rules for Capitalization

- Capitalize the first word in the greeting and closing.
- Capitalize the name of your street, city, state, and country.
- Capitalize the name of the month.
- Capitalize the names of people.
- Capitalize the word *I*.
- Capitalize the first letter of every new sentence.

Rules for Punctuation

- Use a comma (,) after the greeting and closing.
- Use a comma between the city and state.
- Use a comma in the date between the day and the year.
- Use correct end punctuation: period (.), question mark (?), exclamation point (!).

EXERCISE 3

A. Read the letter. Underline the capital letters. Circle the commas.

> 351 Hamilton Parkway
> Harrisburg, PA 10102
> March 30, 2013
>
> Dear Becky,
>
> Thanks so much for your letter. I'm glad you and Ana found a nice apartment. I'm coming to Exton next month. We can see each other then. I'm looking forward to meeting Claudia. She sounds like a great friend. I'll practice my tennis game before I come! Good luck with your classes, and don't work too hard. I'll call you next week and we can plan my visit. Say hello to Ana for me.
>
> Your friend,
> Sarah

B. Compare answers with another student. Are they the same?

A. *Read the letter. Correct the twelve mistakes in capitalization and end punctuation. Add the four missing commas. Then write the corrected letter on a separate piece of paper.*

SOCIAL

32 franklin Street
Phoenix arizona
march 3 2013

dear Sandra

    I just heard the big news about your engagement to sergio. Congratulations! I'm so happy for you. A spring wedding in buenos Aires will be perfect. I know you'll be a beautiful bride

    Things here are fine. The weather is really nice. I go bike riding or hiking every weekend. during the week, I'm busy at work. I got a promotion, and now I'm the office manager

    I'm planning a trip to argentina in july. Is that a good time to visit. Will you be there? Can we meet? Let me know your plans.

        love
        christine

B. *Compare answers with another student. Are they the same?*

Using Contractions in Informal Writing

Contractions are common in speaking. They are also common in informal writing.

A contraction is a short form of two words. It combines two words into one word. Every contraction has an apostrophe (') in it. We put the apostrophe in place of a missing letter or letters. For example, we can combine the two words *are not* into the contraction *aren't*. The apostrophe replaces the letter *o* in *not*.

We often use contractions in sentences with the verb *be*.

Examples:

Affirmative Contractions

*I hope **you are** doing well.*	→	*I hope **you're** doing well.*
***He is** from Russia.*	→	***He's** from Russia.*
***I am** learning to write in English.*	→	***I'm** learning to write in English.*
***What is** your new address?*	→	***What's** your new address?*
***We are** happy to see you.*	→	***We're** happy to see you.*
***They are** leaving soon.*	→	***They're** leaving soon.*

We also use contractions with negative verbs.

Examples:

Negative Contractions

*I **did not** write sooner.*	→	*I **didn't** write sooner.*
*She **is not** a student here.*	→	*She **isn't** a student here.*
*He **is not** in my class.*	→	*He **isn't** in my class.*
*They **do not** speak English.*	→	*They **don't** speak English.*
*My friend **does not** live on campus.*	→	*My friend **doesn't** live on campus.*

> **Note:**
> There are two ways to make contractions with some negative forms of the verb **be**.
>
> | | | |
> |---|---|---|
> | We **are not** | → | We **aren't** or We**'re not** |
> | He (She, It) **is not** | → | He (She, It) **isn't** or He**'s** (She**'s**, It**'s**) **not** |
> | They **are not** | → | They **aren't** or They**'re not** |

A. *Read the letter. Circle the six contractions in the letter.*

SOCIAL

June 4, 2013

Dear Jordan,

Hello from Buffalo. Thanks so much for helping me move here last weekend. You're really a great friend. You're also a great packer! We're a great team! We got all my furniture in the truck. I didn't think it would fit. Most of all, thanks for coming with me. The move was much easier and more fun with you. I hope your back doesn't hurt. Those boxes were very heavy! Tell everyone in Syracuse hello for me. I'll write more soon.

Thanks again,
Paul

B. *Compare answers with another student. Are they the same?*

A. *Rewrite each sentence. Use contractions where possible. Follow the example in number 1.*

1. I hope you are having a good semester.

   I hope you're having a good semester.

2. I am sorry I forgot your birthday.

3. I do not have your new phone number.

4. My grandparents do not have email.

(continued)

5. Janice is not coming to the meeting.

_____

6. I am not in this class.

_____

7. He is from Vietnam.

_____

8. What is your new address?

_____

9. Max does not like to write letters.

_____

10. They are not home.

_____

B. *Compare answers with another student. Are they the same?*

EXERCISE 7

Read Jordan's letter to Paul. Rewrite the letter on a separate piece of paper. Use contractions where possible.

June 10, 2013

Hello Paul,

I hope you are settled into your new apartment. Did you unpack all those boxes yet? I had dinner with Matt and Alisha last night, and they both say hi. They are going to New York this weekend to visit Matt's parents. They do not want to take their dog, so I am keeping him at my apartment for the weekend. I hope he does not scare my cat! My classes start next week. It is hard to believe this is my last year of college. I will call you soon.

Write soon,
Jordan

WRITING TASK

Write a friendly letter.

A. *Prepare for writing. Follow these steps:*

1. Write the name of a friend or family member: _____

2. Write notes about yourself to share with the person you chose in step 1.
Examples:

> *I am meeting new friends.*
> *I start school tomorrow.*
> *I'm getting a promotion at work soon.*

3. Write notes about your plans.
Examples:

> *I'm going to move to a new city.*
> *I want to move to a new apartment.*

B. **Use your notes. Write a letter to your friend or family member on a separate piece of paper.**

C. **Work with a partner. Take turns. Read your letter aloud.**

Check Your Writing

A. *Read your letter in the Writing Task. Use this form to check your letter.*

> ### Friendly Letter Checklist
>
> **The letter . . .**
>
> - has a heading. ☐
> - has a greeting. ☐
> - has a body. ☐
> - has a closing and signature. ☐
> - has correct punctuation and capitalization. ☐
> - has contractions where possible. ☐

B. **Correct any errors in your letter. Then write your letter again.**

POSTCARDS

Many people like to send postcards to their friends and family members when they are traveling or on vacation. A **postcard** is like a short letter. There is not very much room to write on a postcard, so we usually write a few short sentences.

Parts of a Postcard

When you write a postcard, you write your message on the left side of the card. The right side of the postcard is for the address.

These are the parts of a postcard. They are similar to the parts of a letter.

Left Side	Right Side
Date	Name of the person you are writing
Greeting	
Body	Address of the person you are writing
(This part is usually several short sentences.)	
Closing	
Signature	

Remember to include the person's full name, address, and zip code (or postal code). Include the name of the country when you are writing from another country.

Work with another student. Label the parts of a postcard.

SOCIAL

June 12, 2013

Hi Juan,

I'm having a great time in Big Sky, Montana. It snows every day! I met some nice people at the hotel, and we usually ski together. The hotel is OK. It's comfortable and clean and not too expensive. The skiing is fantastic and the views are spectacular!

Wish you were here,

Carlos

Juan Garcia
251 Longest Lane
Philadelphia, PA 19104

Useful Phrases in Postcards

We use informal language when we write postcards. Sometimes we use short phrases instead of complete sentences. The phrases usually include adjectives.

These short phrases are not complete sentences, but you capitalize the first word in the phrase and use the same end punctuation as in a sentence. Sometimes these phrases end in an exclamation point (!) to show excitement.

Useful Phrases

- Having a great time!
- Having a terrible time!

- Perfect weather.
- Awful weather.

- Fantastic food!
- Horrible food!

- Great hotel!
- Shabby hotel!

- Fabulous beaches.
- Spectacular views.
- Terrific nightlife.
- Boring city.

- Friendly people.
- Unfriendly people.

- Wish you were here.
- Say hello to . . .

EXERCISE 9

Read the postcard. There are fourteen mistakes in capitalization and punctuation. Correct the mistakes. Then write the corrected postcard on a separate piece of paper.

feb 12, 2013

Dear nathan,

     having a great time in chicago. friendly people. Amazing food, architecture, and shopping. Unfortunately, it's cold and windy here. i want to come back in the spring. Wish you were here

love
allie

nathan White
25 shorter Street
atlanta GA 31192

Complete the postcards. Use Useful Phrases from the box on page 76.

1

May 3, 2013

Dear Lucy,

Having a _____ time in
San Diego! _____ weather!
_____ beaches. Yesterday
I went surfing for the first time.
We're going to Disneyland tomorrow
and Sea World on Fri.

See you soon,
Stan

2

Oct. 14, 2013

Dear Mom and Dad,

_____ a terrible time!
_____ city. _____
weather. It rains all the time. Our hotel is
OK. _____ people, but good food.

Say hello to Pete and tell him I miss him.

Love,
Andrea

(continued)

3

June 8, 2013

Dear Carol and Dave,

The Smoky Mountains are fantastic! _____ hotel with spectacular views of the mountains. _____ weather! Not hot, not cold, just right. The chef at the hotel is famous. _____ food every night! Today we're going on a hike. Tomorrow we're going fishing.

_____ time! Wish you were here.

Love,
Janet and Carl

WRITING TASK

Write a postcard.

A. *Prepare for writing. Work with another student. Imagine you are on vacation. Look at the postcard on the next page. Talk about your vacation. Use the questions to help you.*

- Where are you? Are you having a good time?
- What is the weather like?
- What interesting things did you see and do?
- Did you meet people on your trip? What are they like?
- Where are you staying?
- Are you enjoying the nightlife?
- Is the food good?

The Beautiful Bahamas!

SOCIAL

B. *Use the ideas from your discussion in Exercise A. Write a postcard to a friend on a separate piece of paper.*

C. *Work in a group. Take turns. Read your postcards aloud.*

Check Your Writing

A. *Read your postcard in the Writing Task. Use this form to check your writing.*

> ### Postcard Checklist
>
> **The postcard . . .**
>
> - has a date. ☐
>
> - has a complete address. ☐
>
> - uses correct capitalization and punctuation. ☐
>
> - has a closing and signature. ☐
>
> - uses informal language. ☐

B. *Correct any errors in your writing. Then write your postcard again.*

In Unit 1 of Part 2, you learned about social writing and practiced writing friendly letters and postcards. Letters and postcards are a traditional type of social writing. They are a type of writing you, your parents, your grandparents, and maybe even your great-grandparents did at some time in the past. Today, many people still write letters and postcards, but they also use new kinds of social writing.

In this unit, you will learn about some other kinds of social writing. You will practice writing emails and blogs. These kinds of social writing are newer. They use the Internet to communicate with family and friends. They make writing to people faster. They make your writing available to more people at one time. And they are excellent ways to practice expressing your ideas in English and sharing them with other people.

For this course, your teacher can make a class blog for you and your classmates to use at **http://pearsonELT.com/writingpowerblog**. On the blog, you and your classmates can practice posting on topics that interest you. You will be able to read each other's posts and make comments on them. See the Introduction to this book for more on how to get started on your *Writing Power 1* class blog.

Warm Up

Work in a group. Discuss these questions:

- Do you use the Internet to communicate with your friends or family members?
- Would you rather write a letter or send an email? Why?
- Do you ever read blogs? Do you have a favorite blog? What is it about?

EMAILS

Emails are a fast and easy way to communicate with friends and family members. Email means electronic mail. Emails are similar to letters, but we send and receive them in a different way. We send email over the Internet.

In order to send an email you need an email address. If you don't have an email address, you can create one. All you need is a computer, a web browser, and an Internet connection.

Discuss these questions with another student:

- Do you have an email address?
- How often do you use email?
- Who do you usually send emails to?
- What kind of emails do you receive?

Parts of an Email

Emails, like friendly letters, usually have five main parts: the heading, greeting, body, closing, and signature. Read the information about the five parts.

Heading

The heading of an email includes several sections.

- **Date and time:** This is the date and time that the email was sent. You do not have to enter this information.

- **From:** This is the name or email address of the sender of the email.

- **To:** This is the name of the receiver of the email. Here, you enter the email address of the person you are sending the email to.

- **cc:** This lists other people who will receive the email. You enter email addresses of any other person you want to receive your email.

- **Subject:** This tells what the email is about. It tells the main reason you are writing the email. It is similar to the title of a paragraph or essay. It is usually very short—just a word or short phrase.

Greeting

Greetings for informal emails are usually short.

> **Examples:**
>
> *Hi [name],*
> *Hey [name],*
> *Hi,* or *Hello, [with no name]*
> *[name],*

Body

The body is the message you want to write. This part is often short, too.

Closing

Closings for informal emails are optional.

> **Examples:**
>
> *Talk to you soon,*
> *See you soon,*
> *Later,*
> *Take care,*
> *Love,*

Signature

The signature is your name. Sometimes you can just type your first name.

Remember

In social writing, you can use informal language and contractions.
(See Part 2, Unit 1, for more on informal language and contractions.)

A. *Read the email. Then discuss these questions with another student:*

1. Who wrote the email?
2. Who received the email?
3. What is the email about?

SOCIAL

From: Beth@mymail.net
To: Stephanie@getmail.com ⎤ *heading*
cc:
Subject: Dinner on Saturday ⎦

Hi Stephanie, ⎤_____

I'm coming to Toronto this weekend. Are you
going to be there? Let's get together. I have big
news. Are you free for dinner on Sat. night?
Let me know and we can make plans.

See you soon, ⎤_____
Beth ⎤_____

B. *Read the email again. Write each part of the email on the lines.*

body   greeting   signature
closing   heading

A. *Read the emails. Circle the best subject and write it on the line.*

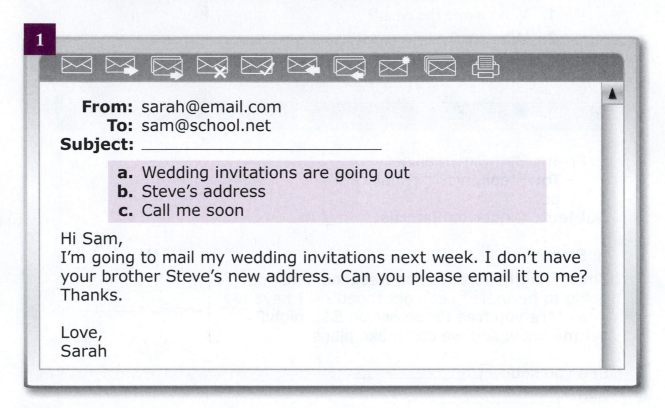

1

From: sarah@email.com
To: sam@school.net
Subject: _____

    a. Wedding invitations are going out
    b. Steve's address
    c. Call me soon

Hi Sam,
I'm going to mail my wedding invitations next week. I don't have your brother Steve's new address. Can you please email it to me? Thanks.

Love,
Sarah

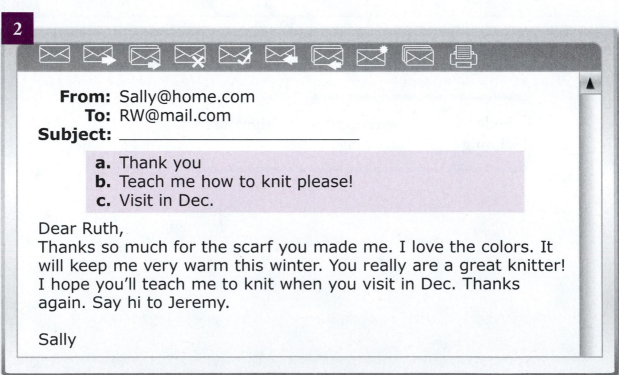

2

From: Sally@home.com
To: RW@mail.com
Subject: _____

    a. Thank you
    b. Teach me how to knit please!
    c. Visit in Dec.

Dear Ruth,
Thanks so much for the scarf you made me. I love the colors. It will keep me very warm this winter. You really are a great knitter! I hope you'll teach me to knit when you visit in Dec. Thanks again. Say hi to Jeremy.

Sally

3

From: GGL@work.com
To: Matt@yourmail.net
Subject: _____

> **a.** Email me
> **b.** Hope you're having a good week
> **c.** Swimming on Sat.?

Hey Matt,
I hope you're having a good week. If you aren't busy on Sat. afternoon, do you want to go swimming with Jason and me? We're planning to go at 9 A.M. at the Walnut Swim Club. I hope you can come. Call me or email me.

Talk to you soon,
Greg

SOCIAL

4

From: lauraw@home.net
To: Cindy12@school.com
Subject: _____

> **a.** Salad recipe
> **b.** Frank's surprise party
> **c.** Thanks for the email

Cindy,
Thanks for your email. We'd love to come to the surprise birthday party for Frank next Sat. Can I bring anything? I can make a salad or an appetizer. Just let me know. Give me a call over the weekend.

See you soon,
Laura

B. *Compare your answers with another student. Are they the same?*

A. *Work with another student. Read the emails. Write a subject on the line.*

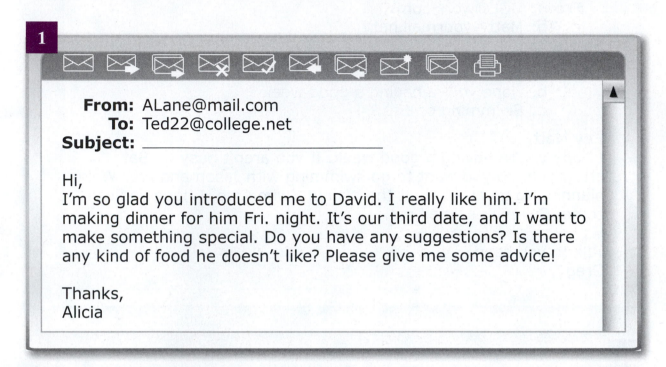

1

From: ALane@mail.com
To: Ted22@college.net
Subject: _____

Hi,
I'm so glad you introduced me to David. I really like him. I'm making dinner for him Fri. night. It's our third date, and I want to make something special. Do you have any suggestions? Is there any kind of food he doesn't like? Please give me some advice!

Thanks,
Alicia

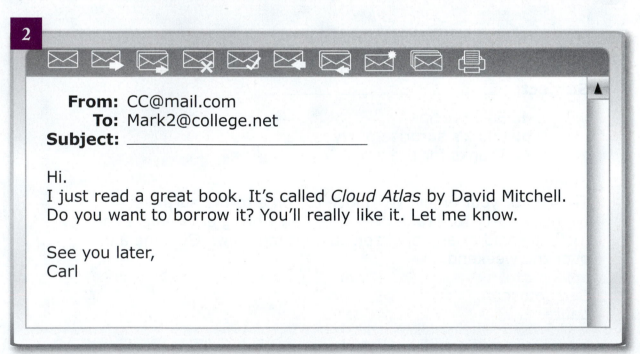

2

From: CC@mail.com
To: Mark2@college.net
Subject: _____

Hi.
I just read a great book. It's called *Cloud Atlas* by David Mitchell. Do you want to borrow it? You'll really like it. Let me know.

See you later,
Carl

3

From: Betsy@mail.com
To: Marcia@univ.net
Subject: _____

Hey Marcia,
I'm looking forward to seeing you this week. Can we change our lunch date from Wed. to Thurs.? We have a lunch meeting at work on Wed. and I can't miss it. I hope Thurs. is OK for you. Let me know.

See you soon,
Betsy

SOCIAL

4

From: Al32@vmail.com
To: Lynn@State.net
Subject: _____

Lynn,
Do you want to go together to Samantha's bridal shower? I can pick you up at your house at 11:30. I have directions to the restaurant. It'll take about 20 minutes to get there from your place. Let me know.

Love,
Alicia

B. *Join another pair. Compare your answers. Which subject best describes each email?*

Using Abbreviations in Informal Writing

An **abbreviation** is a short form of a word. For example, *Sat.* (in the email in Exercise 1A) is the abbreviation for the written word *Saturday*. When you write friendly letters and informal emails, you can use abbreviations for the days of the week and the months of the year. Learn the abbreviations and the full words together. Notice the period at the end of each abbreviation.

Examples:

*See you **Saturday**. → See you **Sat.***

*Her birthday is on **February 3**. → Her birthday is on **Feb. 3**.*

Remember

Capitalize the first letter of the days of the week and the months of the year.

EXERCISE 4

Work with the class. Complete the chart with abbreviations for the days of the week.

Days of the week	Abbreviation
Sunday	Sun.
Monday	
Tuesday	
Wednesday	
Thursday	
Friday	
Saturday	

Work with the class. Complete the chart with abbreviations for months of the year.

Month	Abbreviation	Month	Abbreviation
January	*Jan.*	July	
February		August	
March		September	
April		October	
May		November	
June		December	

SOCIAL

Rewrite the sentences. Use abbreviations for days and months of the year.

1. Let's have lunch on Tuesday.

   Let's have lunch on Tues.

2. I don't have any free weekends in September.

   _____

3. I'll be in New York for two weeks in December.

   _____

4. Can you meet me for dinner on Friday or Saturday?

   _____

5. These pictures are from our vacation last August.

   _____

6. I'm busy all day Wednesday.

   _____

7. She's getting married in October.

   _____

A. **Work with another student. Write an email to your partner on a separate piece of paper.**

- Invite your partner to your house for dinner.
- Include the time and day of the dinner in your email.

B. **Exchange your email with your partner. Read your partner's invitation and write a response.**

C. **Compare your emails. Discuss the ways they are the same and different.**

> ### Remember
>
> Begin each sentence with a capital letter. Use capital letters to begin the names of people, days of the week, months of the year, and streets and cities. Use correct end sentence punctuation.

WRITING TASK

Write an email.

A. **Prepare for writing. Follow these steps:**

1. Choose a classmate. Write your classmate's name: _____
2. Choose one of these ideas to write about, or use your own idea:

   a. Ask the classmate you chose in step 1 for the homework assignment. Ask about the assignment and the due date.
   b. Ask the classmate you chose in step 1 to go to a movie with you. Include the day and time of the movie.

B. **On a separate piece of paper, write an email to your classmate about the topic.**

C. **Work with your classmate. Read your classmate's email. Write an email response on a separate piece of paper.**

Check Your Writing

A. Read your email in the Writing Task. Use this form to check your writing.

> ### Email Checklist
>
> **The email . . .**
>
> - has a short subject line with the main idea. ☐
> - has correct punctuation and capitalization. ☐
> - has contractions where possible. ☐
> - uses abbreviations where possible. ☐

B. Correct any errors in your writing. Then write your email again.

SOCIAL

BLOGS

Every day people communicate online. It is becoming more and more popular. One way to communicate online is emailing. Another popular way to communicate online is blogging.

In this unit you will practice writing short blogs and comments to blog posts. You and your classmates can use the **Writing Power Blog** (http://pearsonELT.com/ writingpowerblog) to practice blog posts throughout this course, or for a time period set by your teacher. (See page vi for more information.)

What Is a Blog?

A **blog** is a place to share information online. The word *blog* is short for "web log." A blog is a special type of website. You can read, write, and share information on a blog. The information is called an entry or a post. A blog usually has many posts. The newest post is at the top of the page.

Blogs are different from other types of websites. On a blog, readers "discuss" the information. They write their ideas and opinions about the blog. Everyone can read their writing. So blogs are another type of social writing.

Who Writes and Reads Blogs?

People who write blogs are called *bloggers*. Bloggers usually write posts on a topic. Then people read the posts and write short comments. Anyone can write a blog. Anyone can read your blog. And anyone can comment on a post.

What Are Some Types of Blogs?

There are many types of blogs. Some blogs are like personal diaries. Others are about politics and news. Still others are about special topics like hobbies, fashion, music, or science. Many blogs include pictures, music, videos, and links to other websites.

Talk about these questions in a small group:

- Do you read blogs in your language?
- Do you read blogs in English?
- Do you have any favorite blogs? What are they? Why do you like them?
- Do you ever write blogs in your language or in English?
- Do you ever write comments on other people's blogs?

Note: Blogging is about sharing ideas with other people online.

EXERCISE 8

A. ***Read the blog post. Then work with another student. Answer the questions.***

HOME   CONTACT ME   ABOUT THIS BLOG   TOP POSTS   SUBSCRIBE

DO YOU HAVE A DAILY ROUTINE?
MAY 30th

My Day

My name is Carolina and I am new at blogging. In fact, this is my first blog. I hope I have time to write every day, but my days are very busy. I am a full-time hairstylist. I'll tell you about my typical day.

Every morning, I get up at 7 o'clock. Then I have breakfast and take a shower. After that, I put on my makeup and get dressed for work. I usually listen to the news on the radio while I get dressed. I leave my apartment at 8 o'clock and walk 5 blocks to the salon. Here's the link to the salon: www.curlsandcuts.com. I often buy a cup of coffee on the way to work. My first appointment is at 8:30. I usually have four clients in the morning. I eat lunch at noon. Sometimes I eat quickly because I have a lot of clients in the afternoon. I finish my last client at 6 o'clock. Then I clean up and sweep the floor. After that, I walk back home and make dinner. I like to relax after dinner and watch TV or read. Finally, I go to sleep at 11 o'clock.

I love my job because it's creative and fun. I also love talking to my clients. Now some of them are my friends! Look at the pictures of some of my favorite haircuts. I'm always looking for new clients. So if you are in the area, come to *Curls and Cuts*!

Leave a Reply
Enter your comment here . . .

Amy 2: *I enjoyed your blog. I'm going to visit Curls and Cuts the next time I need a haircut!*

Jenny 1234: *I liked your blog, and I need some advice. I'm thinking about becoming a hairstylist. Do you think it's a good profession? I like people and I'm creative.*

1. What are some things you learned about Carolina? Check (✓) the true statements. How do you know? Find the answers in the blog.

   ☐ Carolina writes a blog every day.
   ☐ Carolina is a hairstylist.
   ☐ She has a busy schedule.
   ☐ She usually takes the bus to work.
   ☐ Carolina works at night.
   ☐ Carolina thinks her job is fun.

2. What is Carolina's blog mainly about? Circle the answer. How do you know?

   a. Her daily routine
   b. Her hair salon
   c. Her clients and friends

3. Do you think this blog is interesting? Do you want to read more blog posts by Carolina?

B. *Read the comments to Carolina's blog in Exercise A. Do you agree with either of the comments?*

C. *Write your own short comment in the blank* Leave a Reply *box in Exercise A.*

A. Work in a small group. Discuss these questions:

• Do you like to cook? Do you have a favorite recipe?

• Do you share recipes with your friends? How often?

• Do you read any cooking blogs?

B. Read the blog post and the comments.

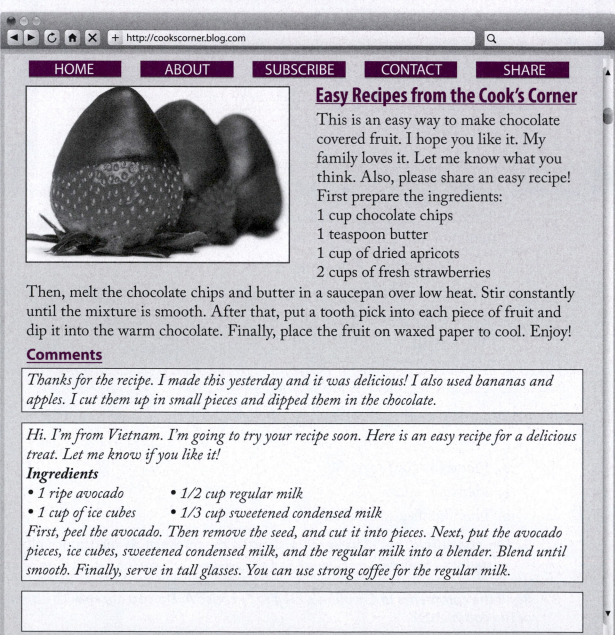

http://cookscorner.blog.com

HOME   ABOUT   SUBSCRIBE   CONTACT   SHARE

Easy Recipes from the Cook's Corner

This is an easy way to make chocolate covered fruit. I hope you like it. My family loves it. Let me know what you think. Also, please share an easy recipe! First prepare the ingredients:

1 cup chocolate chips
1 teaspoon butter
1 cup of dried apricots
2 cups of fresh strawberries

Then, melt the chocolate chips and butter in a saucepan over low heat. Stir constantly until the mixture is smooth. After that, put a tooth pick into each piece of fruit and dip it into the warm chocolate. Finally, place the fruit on waxed paper to cool. Enjoy!

Comments

Thanks for the recipe. I made this yesterday and it was delicious! I also used bananas and apples. I cut them up in small pieces and dipped them in the chocolate.

Hi. I'm from Vietnam. I'm going to try your recipe soon. Here is an easy recipe for a delicious treat. Let me know if you like it!

Ingredients

• *1 ripe avocado*   • *1/2 cup regular milk*

• *1 cup of ice cubes*   • *1/3 cup sweetened condensed milk*

First, peel the avocado. Then remove the seed, and cut it into pieces. Next, put the avocado pieces, ice cubes, sweetened condensed milk, and the regular milk into a blender. Blend until smooth. Finally, serve in tall glasses. You can use strong coffee for the regular milk.

C. Write your own short comment in the blank Comments box in Exercise B.

A. *Read the blog post by an English teacher. Her students read her blog every week. Then they leave comments.*

SOCIAL

Ms. Steven's Blog
"Give Me Five"

Welcome to my blog, *Give Me Five*. This blog is about idioms. English has a lot of idioms, and they are often difficult to learn. Every Monday, I will post five new idioms in my blog. I hope this helps you learn idioms and improve your English. First of all, what is an idiom?

An idiom is a group of words. The group has a special meaning. The meaning of the group of words is different from the meaning of each separate word. For example, "under the weather" is an idiom. It is not about the weather at all. It means "feeling sick or ill."

This week all of the idioms are about numbers. For each idiom, I will give you the meaning and an example sentence.

1. *Give me five.* You say "Give me five." Then you gently hit your open hand against another person's hand. This shows that you are both happy about something.
   • I shouted "Give me five!" to my partner when we beat the other team.
2. *Put two and two together.* This means: you guess the meaning because you heard or saw something.
   • I saw him at her house several times, and I put two and two together. They're dating.
3. *Be on cloud nine.* This means: be very happy about something.
   • I was on cloud nine after I got promoted at work.
4. *Six of one and half a dozen of the other.* This means: two things or situations are almost the same.
   • I like these cameras. I can buy this one or that one and I will be happy. It's six of one and half a dozen of the other.
5. *Go fifty-fifty* (on something). This means: you share the cost of something equally.
   • We went fifty-fifty on our mother's gift. I paid $10.00 and my sister paid $10.00.

I hope this helps you. Do you like to learn idioms this way? Let me know.

B. **Read the comment from one of the students. Then write your own comment in the blank box.**

Leave a Reply

Enter your comment here . . .

> This is a good way to learn idioms. But I think 5 idioms a week are too many. Also, please add more example sentences for each idiom. Thanks!

C. **Share your comment with a partner.**

WRITING TASK

Write a blog about your favorite day.

A. **Prepare for writing. Read the blog post.**

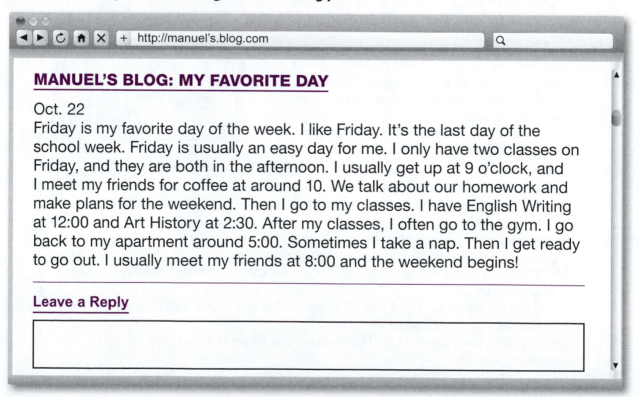

http://manuel's.blog.com

MANUEL'S BLOG: MY FAVORITE DAY

Oct. 22

Friday is my favorite day of the week. I like Friday. It's the last day of the school week. Friday is usually an easy day for me. I only have two classes on Friday, and they are both in the afternoon. I usually get up at 9 o'clock, and I meet my friends for coffee at around 10. We talk about our homework and make plans for the weekend. Then I go to my classes. I have English Writing at 12:00 and Art History at 2:30. After my classes, I often go to the gym. I go back to my apartment around 5:00. Sometimes I take a nap. Then I get ready to go out. I usually meet my friends at 8:00 and the weekend begins!

Leave a Reply

B. **Write a short comment to Manuel in the blank Leave a Reply box.**

C. Complete your own blog about your favorite day.

_____ **BLOG: MY FAVORITE DAY**

_____
(date)

_____ is my favorite day of the week. It's usually a _____

day for me. I _____ get up _____ and then I

_____. After _____, I often _____.

Sometimes, I like to _____. In the evening, I like to

_____. I usually go to bed around _____.

SOCIAL

D. Work with a partner. Share your posts. Write a comment to your partner's post on a separate sheet of paper.

Check Your Writing

A. Read your blog in the Writing Task. Use this form to check your writing.

Blog Checklist

Every sentence in this blog . . .

- begins with a capital letter. ☐
- includes correct punctuation. ☐
- uses contractions where possible. ☐
- uses capital letters for names of people, days, months, cities, and states. ☐

B. Correct any errors in your writing. Then write your blog again.

Further Practice

Blog Topic

- First, write about your least favorite day below or on the Writing Power class blog.

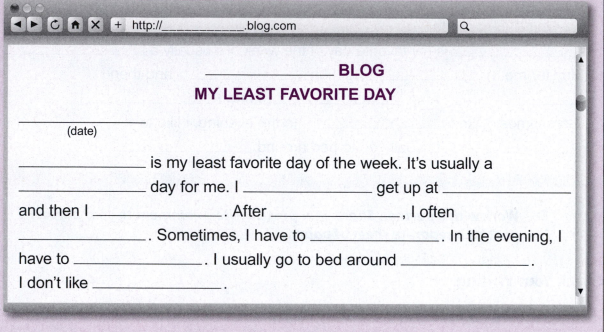

- Write a comment to one of your classmates' blogs.

In Units 1 and 2 of Part 2, you practiced several kinds of social writing. You practiced writing informally about yourself and your ideas. You wrote letters, postcards, emails, and blogs. These are types of writing that you share with other people.

Personal writing is also informal writing about yourself and your ideas. But you usually do not share personal writing with many people. You do personal writing mainly for yourself. Personal writing can be practical or it can be for your own pleasure.

What Is Personal Writing?

- Writing for yourself
- Writing without rules
- Writing reminders or notes to yourself
- Writing to-do lists
- Writing journals or diaries
- Writing as much as you want
- Writing for your own pleasure

Why Is Personal Writing Important?

Personal writing is a great way to practice writing in English. You can do personal writing every day. When you write a little every day, you learn a lot. You learn new words. You can practice different types of sentences. You don't have to worry about someone else reading your writing. You begin to write faster and more clearly. And best of all, you begin to think in English. Personal writing helps you organize and develop your ideas in English.

In this unit, you will practice personal writing in different types of journals:

- Picture journals
- List journals
- Sentence journals
- Topic journals

Work in a group. Look at the picture of a woman writing in her journal. Discuss these questions:

- Why do people enjoy personal writing?
- Do you enjoy personal writing?
- Do you write in a journal or a diary?
- If yes, what kinds of things do you write about?
- If no, what kinds of things do you think you would enjoy writing about?

WHAT IS JOURNAL WRITING?

A **journal** is a special notebook or document on your computer. Think of your journal as a safe and friendly place. In your journal, you can write your ideas, opinions, experiences, and feelings in English.

You can write in your journal every day, a few times a week, or once a week. The important thing is to write regularly!

People use journals in many different ways and for many different reasons. Some people write about things that happen to them during the day. Other people write about things that make them happy or sad. Many people write about their hopes, problems, dreams, or goals. There is no limit to the things you can write about in your journal or the ways you can use your journal.

A. *Read the list of some ways that people use their journals. Check (✓) the activities or types of writing you sometimes do.*

□ To record your ideas, thoughts, and feelings
□ To make lists
□ To write letters to yourself
□ To brainstorm ideas that you can write about later
□ To record things that happen in your life
□ To keep special photographs, souvenirs, cards, invitations, letters, recipes
□ To draw pictures and cartoons
□ To write poems, stories, and songs
□ To think about problems

SOCIAL

B. *Work in small groups. Compare the items you checked.*

C. *What things on the list would you like to do? What things do you think would help you improve your English writing skills?*

WHY IS JOURNAL WRITING IN ENGLISH USEFUL?

Writing regularly in a journal will help you in several ways.

1. **Journal writing helps you become a better writer.**

   The more you write, the better your writing will become. Regular writing can make you a more confident writer. You will see your fluency improve!

2. **Keeping a journal in English helps you think in English.**

   When you write regularly in English in a journal, you begin to think in English.

3. **Journal writing is a good way to try out new language.**

   You can try new words in your journal. This will help you improve your vocabulary.

Work with your class. Answer the question. Make a list.

What other ways can regular journal writing help you?

1. _____

2. _____

3. _____

4. _____

HOW DO YOU DO JOURNAL WRITING?

Before you start a journal, you need to make some decisions. These exercises will help you make some decisions about how you keep a journal in this class.

EXERCISE 3

A. ***Complete the questionnaire. Check (✓) Agree or Disagree.***

	Agree	Disagree
1. I want to write in my journal during class.		
2. I want to write in my journal at home.		
3. I want the teacher to read my journal.		
4. I want my classmates to read my journal.		
5. I want the teacher to choose topics or questions.		
6. I want to write my own list of topics or questions.		
7. I want to write freely, without a certain topic.		
8. I want to write only once a week.		
9. I want to write several times a week.		

B. ***Share your answers with the class. Are they the same?***

A. *Read the tips for keeping a journal. Discuss other tips with your teacher and classmates. Add them to the list.*

- Use a special notebook or computer document. Use it only for your journal.

- Choose a special pen, pencil, colored pencils, markers, computer font. Use it only for your journal writing.

- Write in a comfortable, quiet place. Play soft music.

- Choose a time to write in your journal. Keep a schedule. Make writing in your journal part of your routine.

- On the first page of your journal, write your personal information. You can write your full name, your address, your phone number, your email address, or other information.

- Begin every journal entry the same way: Write the date in the upper right corner of the page. Where are you? Write your location. You can also write the time.

- Write a title for your entry at the top of the page.

- Don't worry about grammar, spelling, or punctuation. Just write.

SOCIAL

Other ideas:

- _____

- _____

- _____

- _____

B. *Work with another student. Discuss these questions:*

- Do you want to write your journal in a notebook? What size and style?

- Do you want to write your journal on your computer, smartphone, or tablet?

- What pen, pencil, or font do you want to use for your journal?

- When do you do want to write? In the morning, after class, during class, in the evening, on weekends?

(continued)

- Where do you want to write? At home? In class? In a park? In the library?

- How often do you want to write in your journal?

- What personal information do you want to write on the first page?

SAMPLE JOURNAL WRITING

Sometimes it is difficult to begin journal writing. What will you write? What words do you know? How can you write your ideas? Practice writing sample journal entries here. It will give you ideas and make you feel comfortable about your writing.

EXERCISE 5

A. Practice writing in a journal. Complete this sample journal entry.

_____
(Today's date)

_____
(Your location)

I am in my English class. There are _____ people in my class. They are from _____ countries. My teacher's name is _____. Today we are learning _____. For me, learning English is _____. The most difficult thing about learning English is _____. The best thing about learning English is _____.

B. Share your journal entry with a partner.

A. *Practice writing in a journal. Complete this sample journal entry. You can use words and phrases from the boxes, or your own words.*

hot	sunny	windy	cloudy
cold	rainy	breezy	gray
warm	stormy	humid	
cool	snowy	mild	

go for a walk	go to the movies	ride my bike
go shopping	make a fire	stay inside
go skiing	rake the leaves	take a nap
go swimming	read a book	watch TV
go to the beach		

SOCIAL

_____
(Today's date)

_____
(Your location)

Today is _____. It is a _____ day. It is _____ outside. I _____ this kind of weather. It is a good day to _____. It's also a good day to _____.

B. *Work in a group. Share journal entries. Did you choose any of the same activities? Which ones?*

A. *Read the sample journal entry below. Underline the words that describe how the student feels.*

Monday, October 3, 2012

Pelham College

10:00 in the morning

Today is Monday. I am happy because it is my 21st birthday. I am thinking about my party tonight. I am excited about my party and celebrating with my friends. I'm sure I'll have a great time. I'm also feeling a little sad because I won't get to celebrate with my family.

B. *Work with your class. Read the list of adjectives that describe different feelings. Add other words that describe feelings.*

Adjectives to Describe Feelings
homesick
glad
nervous
angry
frustrated

C. *Practice writing in a journal. Complete this journal entry. You can use words from the list in Exercise B, and your own words.*

(Today's date)

(Your location)

(The time)

Today is _____. I am _____
(day of week)
because _____. I am thinking
about _____. That makes me
_____.

SOCIAL

WHAT TYPES OF JOURNAL WRITING CAN YOU DO?

Sometimes it is difficult to begin writing. You have lots of ideas. But how can you say them in English? Don't worry! You can begin by drawing a picture or writing a list of words. Then, you can write sentences and paragraphs. There are many different ways to write your ideas in a journal. Here are some types of journals that you can try.

Picture Journals

In a **picture journal**, you start with something visual, for example a picture or a drawing. Then you write a few words or sentences about the picture.

Here are some ideas for a picture journal:

- Draw a picture to show how you feel today. You don't have to be an artist. If you are feeling happy, you can just draw a smiley face.
- Draw a picture of something you did recently.
- Paste a photograph of someone special to you.
- Paste a postcard or picture of a special place.
- Paste a keepsake of something special, for example, a card, notes, or a ticket stub.

Example:

March 10, 2012
St. Louis, Missouri

My son's 5th birthday! A wonderful day.

Draw a picture or paste a photograph of something special you did recently. Write a few words about the picture.

_____

_____

List Journals

Another kind of journal is called a **list journal.** A list journal is fun. You make a list of categories of things. Then you write one or two sentences about one or more items on the list. The lists and sentences can help you think of ideas to write about later.

Here are some ideas for a list journal:

- My favorite foods
- My five favorite movies
- My favorite books
- Five places I want to visit
- Five favorite songs
- Things that make me happy
- Things that make me nervous
- Things that make me proud
- Five things I do well
- Five things I want to learn
- _____
- _____
- _____

SOCIAL

EXERCISE 9

A. *Work in a group. Think of three more ideas for list journals. Add your ideas to the lines above.*

B. *Choose one of the ideas for a list journal from the list above. Write the title of the list and five items in the sample journal on the next page.*

Example:

Things that make me happy:

sunny days

chocolate cake

spending time with my family

the color orange

a good book

(continued)

C. *Write a sentence or two on a separate piece of paper about one of the items on your list.*

Example:

The color orange always makes me happy. It is a bright and cheerful color.

Sentence Journals

Sentence journals are also interesting to write. In a sentence journal, you write one sentence in your journal every day. For example, before you go to bed, you write one sentence about your day.

You can also complete one of these sentences every day.

- Today was a _____ day.

- I am good at _____.

- I like to _____.

- I feel _____ when I _____.

- I don't like to _____.

- My friends think I am _____ and _____.

- I want to learn how to _____ because _____.

Sometimes writing one sentence helps you think of other things to write.

Look at these examples. Two students wrote them in their journals. Both students started with the sentence, "I like to _____."

Examples:

Feb. 8, 2013
Columbia, SC

I like to ride my bike. I feel good outside in the fresh air. Riding my bike every day is a good way to exercise. It helps me stay in shape.

SOCIAL

March 17, 2013
Nashville, TN

I like to cook. Cooking relaxes me. I feel happy when I make something good. Some people don't like to cook, but I think cooking is fun. I enjoy reading cookbooks and trying new recipes.

EXERCISE 10

A. *Write a sentence for your journal on a separate piece of paper. Describe your day or complete one of the sentences from Sentence Journals.*

B. *Read your sentence aloud. Can you think of another sentence or two? Write them in your journal.*

Topic Journals

Writing in a journal is a great way to think about topics. In a **topic journal** you record your ideas about a specific topic. Your teacher can give you a topic, or you can choose one as a class. Read the topic journal entry by a student. Notice the topic at the top of the entry.

Example:

> Topic: Write about a special day in your life
>
> June 21, 2013
> Newtown, Texas
>
> A Special Day
> Yesterday was a special day for my family. My sister had a baby girl! I am very happy. The baby's name is Aya. Aya means colorful. Yesterday was also my sister's birthday. So my sister and her baby have the same birthday. Next year we will have a big party. My sister will be twenty-seven, and my new niece will be one. I am very proud to be an aunt.

EXERCISE 11

Write an entry in your journal. You can write about a special day, or choose a topic of your own.

Letter Journals

In Part 2, Unit 1, you learned about personal letters. You can use your journal as a kind of mailbox. In this mailbox, you can write and keep letters to yourself or letters to other people. You can even write to your teacher. Sometimes it is easier to describe your feelings in a letter than it is in person. And you don't ever need to share the letter.

Read the example letter journal entry. A student wrote this entry to his teacher.

> May 4, 2013
> Oldtown, Texas
>
> Dear Ms. Foster,
>   I am glad you are my English teacher. I like your class a lot. But I have one problem with your class. Sometimes I can't hear you. Can you please talk louder? Thank you.
>
>   Your student,
>   Samuel

EXERCISE 12

Write a letter to your teacher in the sample journal. Tell your teacher something you like or do not like about the class. Then copy the letter into your own journal.

CLASS JOURNAL

In this class, you will keep a journal in English. Look at the exercises and explanations in this unit again and make decisions with your class about your journal writing. There is no right or wrong way to keep a journal. The goal is to write a lot, to write regularly, and to write your ideas confidently in English.

EXERCISE 13

Work with your classmates and your teacher. Discuss these questions. When you reach a decision, write the answers.

1. How often will you write in your journal?

   _____

2. Will you write in class, at home, or both?

   _____

3. Who will choose the topics?

   _____

4. Who will read your journal?

   _____

WRITING TASK

Begin writing in your journal.

A. *Prepare for writing. Follow these steps:*

1. Write today's date and the location. You may also include the time on your journal entry page.

2. Choose the topic of your journal entry and write a title on your journal entry page. Here are some ideas to help you start thinking and writing.

   • Describe your best friend.

   • Write about your favorite kind of music.

   • Write about a big decision you made.

- Describe your favorite movie or book.

- What makes you angry? Happy? Nervous?

- Write about your favorite room in your home.

- Describe your favorite holiday.

- Write about a memory from your childhood.

- What is your favorite kind of weather? Why? What do you like to do in that kind of weather?

- Why are you learning English?

- What do you miss about your country?

- What is your favorite website? Why do you like it?

3. Choose a type of journal writing for your first journal entry, for example, a letter journal, a list journal, or a sentence journal.

B. ***Write your first journal entry in your journal notebook or computer document.***

Further Practice

Journal Ideas

- In Exercise 13, you and your classmates discussed journal writing in this class. Read the decisions you made.

- Continue to write in your journal. Choose another type of journal writing. Write your next journal entry.

Academic Writing

In Part 2 you learned about informal social and personal writing. In Part 3, you will learn about a different type of writing called academic writing. Academic writing is formal writing that you do for school. It is usually different from social and personal writing. It has a different format, sometimes a different sentence structure, and often different topics. It follows certain rules. Some examples of academic writing are book reports and paragraphs about an assigned topic.

Most academic writing includes paragraphs. In this unit and in the rest of Part 3, you will practice writing paragraphs in English. You will learn about:

- The format of a paragraph
- The parts of a paragraph
  - ○ Topic sentences
  - ○ Body sentences
  - ○ Concluding sentences
- The patterns of organization of a paragraph

Warm Up

A. *Work in a group. Look at these types of writing. Are they formal or informal? Write "F" (formal) or "I" (informal).*

_____ **a.** Friendly letters   _____ **f.** A movie review

_____ **b.** A college application   _____ **g.** Greeting cards

_____ **c.** A news article   _____ **h.** A class assignment

_____ **d.** Postcards   _____ **i.** _____

_____ **e.** Blogs   _____ **j.** _____

B. *Add one more example of formal and informal writing to the list.*

C. *Compare answers with another student. Are they the same?*

WHAT IS A PARAGRAPH?

A **paragraph** is a group of sentences. All of the sentences are about one topic. One sentence usually tells the topic. This sentence is the **topic sentence**. It is often the first sentence in the paragraph. In a well-written paragraph, the topic sentence and all the other sentences are about *the same topic*.

Example:

> Green is my favorite color. I think green is a relaxing color. I painted my bedroom light green. I like to wear green clothes. Most of my shirts and sweaters are green. My car is green too. Green reminds me of nature. I love green trees and green grass. I love the color green.

The topic is: *Green*

The topic sentence is: *Green is my favorite color.*

This is a successful paragraph. All the sentences are about the same topic. They tell why green is the writer's favorite color.

Now read this group of sentences.

> Colors have different meanings in different countries. My husband's favorite color is green. Green is the color of nature. People around the world are trying to "go green." Blue is a relaxing color. Red is good luck in China. Many flags use red.

The topic is: *Colors*

The topic sentence is: *Colors have different meanings in different countries.*

This is not a successful paragraph. The topic sentence is: *Colors have different meanings in different countries.* But the sentences are not about this topic. They are about many different topics: *my husband, nature, "go green", blue, red, flags.*

EXERCISE 1

A. Read these groups of sentences. Are all the sentences in each group about the same topic? Write "S" (same topic) or "D" (different topics).

_____ **1.** My favorite color is yellow. Yellow reminds me of the sun. I think yellow is cheerful. My kitchen is yellow. The outside of my house is yellow, too. My favorite sneakers are bright yellow. I love the color yellow.

_____ **2.** Eight is a lucky number in Japan. There are seven people in my family. I think some numbers are lucky and other numbers are unlucky. Many people believe thirteen is an unlucky number. Friday the 13th is an unlucky day. Don't start a trip on a Friday.

_____ **3.** I like to travel. One time I lost my passport. Sometimes, it is difficult to do business in another country. It is fun to try different kinds of food. I love Mexican food. My father travels a lot for his job.

_____ **4.** I like to visit different countries. I like to see how people live in other countries. I like to hear different languages. I also like to try the food in different countries. Most of all, I love meeting new people from all around the world.

B. Compare answers with another student. Are they the same?

C. Work with your class. Look at the groups of sentences in Exercise A again. The sentences marked "S" are successful paragraphs. What is the topic of each paragraph?

PARAGRAPH FORMAT

A paragraph in English has a special format. When you write a paragraph, you need to think about the way it looks. Follow these guidelines.

Guidelines for Paragraphs

- Indent the first sentence of a paragraph. Begin the first word five spaces from the left margin.

- Begin each sentence with a capital letter. End each sentence with a period, question mark, or exclamation point.

- Do not begin each new sentence on a new line. Every sentence in the paragraph follows the sentence before it.

- Do not break words at the end of a line. Move the word to the next line.

For class assignments, you can follow these guidelines, or follow the guidelines your teacher gives you.

- Include a heading: Write your name, the date, and the course title in the upper left corner.

- Leave a one inch margin (blank space) on the right and left side of the paper.

- Sometimes your teacher will ask you to skip lines. Use double-spacing on a computer. Leave a line between each line you handwrite. This makes your writing easier to read and to correct.

- Include a title. Write the title above the paragraph. Center it over the paragraph.

Work with another student. Label the parts of the paragraph. Use the words from the box.

Course title	Indent	Name
Date	Margin	Title of the Paragraph

Julia Scott]_____

July 16, 2013]_____

English Writing 101]_____

My Favorite Color]_____

indent [My favorite color is green. I think green is

a relaxing color. I painted my bedroom light green.

I like to wear green clothes. Most of my shirts

and sweaters are green. My car is green, too.

Green reminds me of nature. I love green trees

and green grass. I love the color green.

A. **Work with the class. Look at the paragraph on page 123. Find the mistakes in the paragraph format. (Use the guidelines on page 121.) Discuss the questions.**

1. Did the writer indent the first sentence?

2. Does every sentence in the paragraph follow the sentence before it?

3. Did the writer leave margins?

4. Did the writer include a title in the correct place?

5. Did the writer include the heading in the correct place?

6. Did the writer break any words at the end of a line?

7. Did the writer use correct punctuation and capitalization?

Linda Frommer

September 12, 2013

English Writing 101

Classroom Customs in the United States

Students in the United States follow several basic classroom customs.
First of all, students should call their teachers by their last name and use
"Mr." or "Ms." in front of it, for example, "Mr. Jones." Sometimes students use
the teacher's first name.

The teacher tells them if that is OK. But students never call their tea
cher "teacher."
    Secondly, students should participate in class. They ask questions and
give opinions. In addition, students should always be polite.
For example, they should turn off cell phones, be on time, and not chew gum in
class.
        Finally, students should never copy another student's test or paper.

B   *Correct the mistakes in the paragraph. Rewrite it on a separate piece of paper.*

C.   *Compare your paragraph with another student. Are they the same?*

A. *Correct the mistakes in the sentences. Add capital letters and end punctuation. Follow the example in number 1.*

1. T̲ipping is important in the United States.

2. in a restaurant, you should leave your server 15 to 20 percent of your bill

3. you do not need to tip in fast food restaurants

4. taxi drivers expect a 10 to 20 percent tip

5. tip people who carry your luggage at airports and hotels

6. the usual tip is $1 per piece of luggage

7. most people tip hairdressers 15 to 20 percent, too

8. tipping is very important, so you should ask for tipping advice

B. *Use the sentences in Exercise A to write a paragraph on a separate piece of paper. Use the title "Tipping Customs in the United States." Use correct paragraph format.*

C. *Compare paragraphs with another student. Are they the same?*

PARTS OF A PARAGRAPH

Most paragraphs have three main parts.

1. The Topic Sentence

The first part is the topic sentence. The topic sentence tells the reader what the paragraph is about.

2. The Body

The second part is the body of the paragraph. This part gives the reader information about the topic. The sentences in the body are called *supporting sentences*. All the supporting sentences must relate to the topic of the paragraph.

3. The Concluding Sentence

The concluding sentence comes after supporting sentences. It is usually the last sentence of the paragraph. The concluding sentence reminds the reader about the topic of the paragraph.

In this unit, you will practice the first part: topic sentences. In the next unit you will learn more about supporting and concluding sentences.

Label the three parts of the paragraph. Write the names of the parts on the lines.

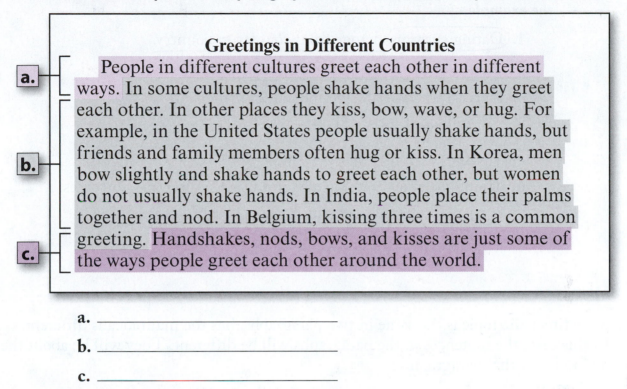

Greetings in Different Countries

a. People in different cultures greet each other in different ways. In some cultures, people shake hands when they greet each other. In other places they kiss, bow, wave, or hug. For example, in the United States people usually shake hands, but friends and family members often hug or kiss. In Korea, men **b.** bow slightly and shake hands to greet each other, but women do not usually shake hands. In India, people place their palms together and nod. In Belgium, kissing three times is a common **c.** greeting. Handshakes, nods, bows, and kisses are just some of the ways people greet each other around the world.

a. _____

b. _____

c. _____

TOPIC SENTENCES

In most paragraphs, the first sentence is **the topic sentence**. The topic sentence is very important. It has two parts: the **topic** and **main idea** of the paragraph. The topic tells what the paragraph is about. The main idea tells what you will say about the topic.

Example:

Topic sentence: *Students in the United States follow several basic classroom customs.*

Topic: *Students in the United States*

Main idea: *They follow several basic classroom customs.*

The topic sentence tells the reader that the paragraph will be about **students in the United States**. The sentences in the paragraph will be about **classroom customs they follow**. The topic sentence controls the rest of the sentences in the paragraph. So, this paragraph will not talk about classroom customs in different countries, or other kinds of customs students in the United States follow.

All of the sentences in the paragraph are about the main idea. A good topic sentence keeps your focus on the topic *and* the main idea.

Circle the topic in each topic sentence. Underline the main idea. Follow the examples.

1. (Dating customs) change from country to country.

2. There are many ways to (celebrate birthdays.)

3. Harvest festivals are common all over the world.

4. Colors have different meanings in different countries.

5. Wedding customs vary around the world.

6. Traditions about naming a baby are similar in some countries.

7. There are several advantages to living in a big city.

8. The library is a good place to study.

Main Idea

Sometimes the topic is the same in two paragraphs, but the main idea is different. In this case, the sentences in the paragraphs will be different. They will be about the main idea of that paragraph.

Examples:

The topic of both these topic sentences is *koalas*, but the main idea about the topic is different.

            Topic   Main idea

Topic sentence: *Koalas are in danger.*

This topic sentence tells the reader the following:

- The paragraph will be about koalas. (topic)
- The sentences in the paragraph will describe how and why koalas are in danger (main idea about the topic). It will not give other information about koalas.

            Topic   Main idea

Topic sentence: *Koalas are cute furry animals.*

This topic sentence tells the reader the following:

- The paragraph will be about koalas. (topic)
- The sentences in the paragraph will describe what koalas look like (main idea about topic). It will not give other information about koalas.

A. *Work with another student. Read the paragraphs. They are all about koalas. Choose a topic sentence for each paragraph. Use the sentences from the box.*

> Koalas are cute furry animals.
> Koalas are in danger.
> Koalas have interesting behaviors.
> Koalas need eucalyptus trees.

Paragraph 1

_____ They live in Australia. Koalas look like teddy bears, but they are not bears. They are marsupials. (Marsupials are a special kind of animal. Mother marsupials carry their babies in a pouch.) Koalas have soft, gray and white fur. They also have a large head with big, furry ears and a wide, flat nose. I think koalas are adorable.

(continued)

Mother koala with a baby in her pouch

Paragraph 2

_____ Koalas live in eucalyptus trees. They live high in the tops of the trees. This keeps them safe from other animals. They move from tree to tree at night. Koalas also eat eucalyptus leaves. They need to eat a lot of eucalyptus leaves to live. Koalas rarely drink water because they get the water they need from eucalyptus leaves. Koalas cannot live without eucalyptus leaves.

Paragraph 3

_____ Koalas are nocturnal animals. They move around and eat at night. Koalas sleep during the day. They usually sleep 16 hours a day. They are arboreal animals. That means that they live in trees. They like to be alone.

Paragraph 4

_____ First of all, koalas are losing their homes. Koalas live in eucalyptus trees, and people are cutting down the trees to build cities and farms. Many koalas are dying, too. They are dying in forest fires and from diseases. In addition, every year cars hit and kill many koalas. Dogs attack and kill koalas, too. Luckily, people around the world are helping to save the koalas.

B. *Join another pair. Compare topic sentences. Are they the same?*

EXERCISE 8

A. **Work with another student. Read the paragraphs on the next page. They are all about sleep. Choose a topic sentence for each paragraph. Use the sentences from the box.**

> Some animals sleep more than others.
> The amount of sleep you need depends mainly on your age.
> There are several ways to get a good night's sleep.
> There are two main kinds of sleep.

Paragraph 1

_____ Newborn babies (up to two months) need the most sleep. They need 12 to 18 hours of sleep per day. Infants (three months to one year old) need about 15 hours of sleep. Preschool children often need 14 hours of sleep. Teenagers need about 8.5 to 10 hours. But many older people need less sleep. They only need about 7 or 8 hours of sleep each night. That's a big difference!

Paragraph 2

_____ One kind is called quiet sleep, and the other is called rapid eye movement (REM) sleep. Every night, you have several periods of quiet sleep and several periods of REM sleep. Most dreaming happens during REM sleep. During REM sleep, your eyes move back and forth rapidly, but no other muscles in your body move. Scientists think deep REM sleep helps your body feel rested in the morning.

Paragraph 3

_____ First of all, you should go to bed at the same time every night, even on weekends and holidays. Also, you should keep your bedroom quiet, dark, and comfortable. The temperature should not be too hot or too cold. There are some things you should avoid, too. Do not drink coffee or tea before bed. Also, do not exercise or watch exciting TV shows before bed. Finally, if all these things fail, you can always count sheep!

Paragraph 4

_____ Giraffes do not need very much sleep. They usually sleep about 2 hours a day. Horses do not sleep very much either. They usually sleep about 3 hours per day. Humans need an average of 8 hours of sleep. Dogs sleep about 10 hours a day. Cats and mice sleep for about 12 hours. Squirrels usually sleep 15 hours a day, and tigers get about 16 hours of sleep. Bats sleep a lot. They often sleep 20 hours a day.

B. _Join another pair. Compare topic sentences. Are they the same?_

A. Read the paragraphs. Choose the best topic sentence for each paragraph. Write the topic sentence on the line.

Paragraph 1

_____ In China, we often give gifts to friends and relatives. We usually give gifts when we visit someone and on holidays and birthdays. Food and tea are common gifts. When we give someone a gift, we use two hands, but it is not polite to open a gift in front of the person. When we receive a gift, we do not send a thank you card. We usually give the person a gift in return. In China, gift giving is very important.

a. Food is a good gift in China.

b. Gifts are important in Chinese culture.

c. Chinese people do not send thank you cards.

Paragraph 2

_____ In some countries, such as Germany and Japan, it is very important to be on time. It is rude to be a few minutes late. In other countries, like the United States and Sweden, people try to be on time, but it is all right to be a few minutes late. In still other countries, such as Norway and France, you can be up to 30 minutes late. Finally, in some places like Brazil and many Middle Eastern countries, being on time is not very important. Most people in these countries will not be angry if you arrive an hour late. So, if you plan to visit another country, you should learn about the customs of time in that country.

a. Customs about time differ around the world.

b. It is always important to be on time.

c. It is interesting to learn about customs.

Paragraph 3

_____ It is a huge, beautiful park in the middle of downtown Sydney, Australia. There are over 7,500 different kinds of plants and a lot of animals. There are magnificent trees, incredible plants, and beautiful flowers. You can see butterflies, owls, and huge bats hanging from trees. It's a great place to relax and learn about plants and animals. It's also a perfect place to have a picnic or take a long walk.

a. Sydney, Australia, is my favorite city.

b. I enjoy learning about plants and animals.

c. The Royal Botanic Gardens is a wonderful place to visit.

Paragraph 4

_____ First of all, Best Beans has the best coffee in town. Every day the owner makes a different type of coffee. He also makes delicious homemade cookies and soups. In addition, the atmosphere is cozy and relaxed. Best Beans feels like a home away from home. There is good music, free Internet, and lots of newspapers and magazines for customers to read. I really like meeting my friends at Best Beans.

a. It is easy to make a good cup of coffee.

b. Our neighborhood coffee shop, Best Beans, is a great place to go.

c. Our neighborhood has many good coffee shops.

B. _Compare answers with another student. Are they the same?_

A. *Work with another student. Write a topic sentence for each paragraph. (Hint: Use the concluding sentence for help.)*

Paragraph 1

_____ She has blue eyes and usually wears blue clothes. Maria thinks blue is a calm color. Her bedroom and living room are blue. She drives a blue car. Maria likes blue skies and the blue ocean. She thinks blue is the most beautiful color.

Paragraph 2

_____ First of all, you can eat at one of Reykjavík's excellent restaurants. You can also visit the museums and theaters. The center of the city has many stores, hotels, and outdoor pools. Best of all, Reykjavík has an exciting nightlife. You can listen to live music at clubs and concerts. Reykjavík is a great city.

Paragraph 3

_____ For example, in Korea, the harvest festival is called Chusok. Koreans visit their hometowns and have a big feast. In the United States, the harvest holiday, Thanksgiving, is also a time for families to get together for a big dinner. In China and Vietnam, people give thanks for the harvest with feasts and celebrations. They eat moon cakes and round fruits. They are symbols of togetherness. In India, the harvest celebration, Pongal, is very important. Like in many other countries, families gather for a big meal and give thanks for a successful harvest. Harvest holidays are celebrated all over the world.

Paragraph 4

_____ During the week Bob works as a bank teller at a large bank. He enjoys his job at the bank and likes his coworkers and customers. On the weekends Bob works for his friend's small photography company. He takes photographs at weddings and other celebrations. Bob really enjoys working as a photographer. He meets lots of people and gets to go to lots of parties. Bob doesn't mind having two jobs.

B. *Join another pair. Talk about your topic sentences. Are they similar?*

Titles

A **title** tells the topic of your writing in a few words. It makes your reader interested in your writing. A title is usually a single word or a short phrase. It is usually not a complete sentence. When you write formally, you often need to write a title.

Follow these guidelines when you write a title.

Guidelines for Titles

- Capitalize the first letter of the first and last word in the title.

- Capitalize the first letter of any other important words in the title.

- Do not capitalize every letter in the title.

- Do not capitalize a preposition (*by, on, at,* etc.) unless it is the first or last word in the title.

- Do not capitalize an article *(a, an, the)* unless it is the first word in the title.

- Do not use a period at the end of the title.

EXERCISE 11

Correct the titles. Follow the example in number 1.

1. my favorite color

   My Favorite Color

2. Dating Customs In The United States.

   _____

3. THE MOST IMPORTANT DAY OF MY LIFE

   _____

4. a Boring Job

   _____

5. It is easy to make rice.

   _____

6. jobs of the Future

   _____

Work with another student. Read the paragraphs. Add a title. Choose a title from the box.

> A Funny Friend   A Terrible Trip
> A Picky Eater   My Amazing Vacation

1. _____

My friend John is very funny. First of all, he tells the best jokes. Every time I see him, John tells me a new joke. He also does great imitations. He can speak and act just like the person he is imitating. Finally, John tells very funny stories. Everyone laughs at his stories. I like to be around John when I'm feeling sad because he always makes me smile.

2. _____

My trip to Iceland was amazing. Iceland has beautiful scenery. There are amazing hiking trails all around Iceland. It has hot springs, glaciers, and volcanoes. I saw whales and went fishing. I went horseback riding, too. Iceland is a great place for a vacation.

3. _____

My trip to San Francisco was a disaster. I went to meet my boyfriend's parents for the first time. I was very excited to meet them and see San Francisco. As soon as I arrived, I started to feel sick. I had a fever, and I felt weak. The next day I had the flu. I spent the whole week in bed. I was sick and very embarrassed.

4. _____

My husband Tomas is a picky eater. For one thing, he hates onions and garlic. He refuses to eat anything that has either of these foods. In addition, there are only a few vegetables that he will eat. He only likes peas and carrots. Finally, Tom hates to try any new kind of food. If I make something new or different, he complains and often won't even try it.

WRITING TASK

Write a paragraph about classroom customs.

A. Prepare for writing. Follow these steps:

1. Work in a group. Discuss classroom customs in your culture.
   a. Do you follow special classroom customs in your country?
   b. What do you call your teacher?
   c. Do you stand up when your teacher enters the classroom?
   d. Do you usually talk in class?
   e. Does your teacher usually do all of the talking?
   f. Can you eat, drink, or chew gum in class?
   g. Can you use your cell phone, computer, or tablet in class?
   h. What are some other customs?

2. Write your own answers to the questions. Write complete sentences.
   Example:
   a. Students in the United States follow special classroom customs.

   a. _____

   b. _____

   c. _____

   d. _____

   e. _____

   f. _____

   g. _____

   h. _____

B. Write your sentences in Exercise A in a paragraph. Write your paragraph on a separate piece of paper. Include a title.

C. Work with a partner. Take turns. Read your paragraphs aloud.

Check Your Writing

A. *Read your paragraph in the Writing Task. Use this form to check your writing.*

> ### Paragraph Checklist
>
> **The paragraph . . .**
>
> - has correct paragraph format. ☐
> - has a topic sentence. ☐
> - has a main idea in the topic sentence. ☐
> - has only complete sentences. ☐
> - has correct punctuation and capitalization. ☐
> - has a correct title. ☐

B. *Correct any errors in your paragraph. Then write your paragraph again.*

Further Practice

Journal or Blog Topic
- Write a paragraph about greetings in your country. Teach your readers how to say hello in your language.

Project Idea
- Make a poster with a list of rules for your class. Display the poster in your classroom.

In Part 3, Unit 1, you learned about topic sentences. The topic sentence tells the topic and the main idea about the topic. It is usually the first sentence of a paragraph. All of the other sentences in the paragraph tell something about the main idea. These sentences form the **body** of the paragraph. The sentences in the body of the paragraph are the **supporting sentences**. The last sentence in the paragraph usually repeats the main idea from the topic sentence. This is the **concluding sentence**.

In this unit, you will practice writing supporting and concluding sentences.

Warm Up

Work in a group. Talk about your favorite season. Answer these questions:

- Where do you live? How many seasons do you have there?
- What is your favorite season?
- What is the weather like in that season?
- What do you like to do in that season?

Spring   Summer

Winter   Fall

SUPPORTING SENTENCES

Supporting sentences follow the topic sentence in a paragraph. Most paragraphs have at least three supporting sentences. Supporting sentences are important because they explain the topic sentence with details, facts, and examples.

Example:

> *Winter is my favorite season. I love to watch the snow falling. Snow covers my garden, and the trees look beautiful. I also love the cold air in winter. The winter air gives me energy. I also love winter clothes, like sweaters and coats.*

In this paragraph, the topic sentence is *Winter is my favorite season.*

The topic is *winter.*

The main idea is *my favorite season.*

There are five supporting sentences. Each supporting sentence gives examples and details about the main idea. They explain *why the writer's favorite season is winter.*

EXERCISE 1

A. Read the paragraphs. Underline the topic sentence. Circle the topic. Double underline the main idea. Count the number of supporting sentences.

Paragraph 1

Fall is the best season to visit Taipei. In fall, the skies are sunny most of the time. There is less rain than other times of the year. The temperature is pleasant. It is usually in the mid-70s Fahrenheit (mid-20s C). There is less humidity than in other seasons, so you feel more comfortable.

Number of supporting sentences: _____

Paragraph 2

Taipei is a city that never sleeps. In Taipei, there is something to do 24 hours a day. Many Internet cafés, tea shops and coffeehouses, and movie theaters stay open all day and all night. The famous night markets are great places to go, too. You can shop, eat, or socialize with your friends all night. Some gyms and bookstores stay open, too.

Number of supporting sentences: _____

Paragraph 3

Beijing has four seasons. Spring (April to May) is often windy and dry with some strong sandstorms. Beijing summers (June to August) are very hot with a lot of rain. In the fall (September to October), there is a lot of sunshine and cooler temperatures. The days and nights are comfortable in the fall. Winters (November to March) are very cold. The temperature often falls below 0 degrees Fahrenheit (–17C), and sometimes it snows.

Number of supporting sentences: _____

B. *Work in groups. Answer the questions about the paragraphs in Exercise A.*

1. In Paragraph 1, the topic sentence is *Fall is the best season to visit Taipei.* Why is fall the best season to visit Taipei? Give four reasons.

   _____   _____

   _____   _____

2. In Paragraph 2, the topic sentence is *Taipei is a city that never sleeps.* Why does the writer say Taipei never sleeps? Give examples.

   _____

   _____

3. In Paragraph 3, the topic sentence is *Beijing has four seasons.* What are the four seasons in Beijing like? Describe them.

   _____   _____

   _____   _____

A. *Read the two topic sentences. Find sentences to support each one. Label the supporting sentences "1" or "2".*

Topic Sentences

1. I love everything about summer.

2. Summer is my least favorite season.

Supporting Sentences

_1_ **a.** When it is warm and sunny, I feel happy.

_2_ **b.** I hate hot weather.

____ **c.** When it is very hot outside, I don't have much energy.

____ **d.** I have a lot of energy in the summer, and I love to be outdoors.

____ **e.** I love skiing and snowboarding, but I cannot do them in the summer.

____ **f.** My favorite sports are surfing and tennis, and they are both summer sports.

____ **g.** I also love summer foods like tomatoes from the garden and, of course, ice cream.

____ **h.** I look forward to summer all year.

____ **i.** I hate bugs, and there are lots of bugs in the summer.

____ **j.** I like all seasons better than summer.

B. *Look at the supporting sentences in Exercise A. Answer the questions.*

1. How many supporting sentences are there for topic sentence 1? ____

2. How many supporting sentences are there for topic sentence 2? ____

C. *Choose one of the topic sentences in Exercise A. Write a paragraph with the topic sentence and supporting sentences. Write it on a separate piece of paper. Use correct paragraph format.*

D. *Compare paragraphs with another student. Are they the same?*

EXERCISE 3

A. *Work with a partner. Look at the pictures. Read the topic sentences. Write three supporting sentences for each.*

1. Topic Sentence: Tom is dressed for summer.

   a. Supporting sentence: _____

   _____

   b. Supporting sentence: _____

   _____

   c. Supporting sentence: _____

   _____

2. Topic Sentence: Paula is ready for winter weather.

   a. Supporting sentence: _____

   _____

   b. Supporting sentence: _____

   _____

   c. Supporting sentence: _____

   _____

B. *Join another pair. Compare your supporting sentences. Are they similar?*

Irrelevant Sentences

All the supporting sentences in a paragraph are about the topic and the main idea in the topic sentence. When you write a paragraph in English, only include sentences about the main idea. Sentences that are not about the topic and the main idea are **irrelevant**. Do not include irrelevant sentences in your paragraphs.

Example:

> *My hometown Jamesville is a great place to live. It is clean and safe. There is not a lot of crime. There are a lot of parks and green places. There are many good restaurants and interesting small shops downtown.* [~~Unfortunately, houses in Jamesville are very expensive.~~] *Best of all, Jamesville has a great school system with excellent teachers, so there are many families with young children.* [~~Melrose is also a great place to live.~~]

- The topic is *Jamesville*.
- The main idea is *Jamesville is a great place to live*.
- Two of the supporting sentences are NOT about *Jamesville* or *a great place to live*. They are irrelevant, so they are crossed out. They do not belong in this paragraph.
  - *Unfortunately, houses in Jamesville are very expensive* is not about why Jamesville is a great place to live.
  - *Melrose is also a great place to live* is not about Jamesville. It is about a different place.

All the other sentences tell why Jamesville is a great place to live.

EXERCISE 4

A. Read the paragraph. Then answer the questions.

Janie is very careful with her money. She always looks in several stores before she buys something. She also checks online and makes sure she is getting a good price. She tries to eat at home often to save money. Janie is careful about the money she spends on entertainment, too. She looks for free concerts and movies.

1. What is the topic of the paragraph? _____

2. What is the main idea of the paragraph? _____

3. Which sentence can you add to the paragraph? Circle the letter. (Hint: The sentence must be about the topic and the main idea.)

   a. She goes to the museum on Sunday when it is free, too.

   b. Janie's brother is also careful with his money.

   c. Janie is a careful driver, too.

B. Discuss this question with the class: Why are the other two sentences in item 3 irrelevant?

**A. Read the paragraph. Underline the topic.
Circle the main idea.**

The ostrich is a special bird in several ways. First of all, it is the world's largest and heaviest bird. Secondly, ostriches cannot fly, but they can run very fast on their strong legs. In fact, ostriches can run 43 miles (70 km) per hour. ~~Another bird, the peregrine falcon, is the fastest animal in the world.~~ The ostrich has the largest eyes of any land animal. Each eye is about 2 inches (5 cm) across. It is the only bird with only two toes on its feet. The ostrich's egg is also the biggest egg in the world. ~~Many ostriches live in Africa.~~

B. Work with another student. Look at the sentences that are crossed out.

1. Why is this sentence irrelevant? *Another bird, the peregrine falcon, is the fastest animal in the world.*

_____

2. Why is this sentence irrelevant? *Many ostriches live in Africa.*

_____

3. Which sentence can you add to the paragraph? Circle the letter. Discuss your answer.
(Hint: The sentence must be about the topic and the main idea.)

   a. Ostriches live in groups of five to fifty birds.
   b. I really like ostriches.
   c. The hummingbird's egg is the smallest egg in the world.

A. **Read the paragraphs. For each paragraph, underline the topic sentence. Circle the main idea. Cross out the irrelevant sentence.**

Paragraph 1

There are many types of blogs. Some blogs are like personal diaries. People write about their daily lives or about family events. Other blogs are less personal. They are about politics and news. Newspapers also have articles about national politics. Still other blogs are about special topics like hobbies, fashion, music, or travel. Many of these blogs include pictures, music, videos, and links to other websites.

Paragraph 2

People eat different parts of plants. For example, people eat lettuce and spinach. They are the plant's leaves. Celery and asparagus are the stems of the plant. We eat the fruit of tomato and squash plants. We can also buy canned vegetables and frozen vegetables. Beans, corn, and peas are seeds that we eat. When we eat radishes or carrots, we are eating roots. We also eat the flowers of cauliflower and broccoli plants.

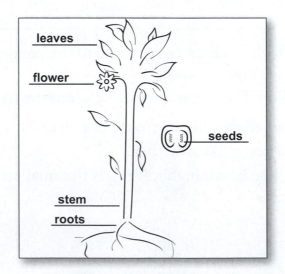

Paragraph 3

People around the world celebrate International Peace Day on September 21. The United Nations (UN) created International Peace Day in 1981. The first Peace Day celebrations were in September 1982. For the next twenty years, people celebrated International Peace Day on the third Tuesday of September. But in 2002, the UN General Assembly changed the date. It officially named September 21 the permanent date for the yearly celebration. There are several other holidays in September. Now people in countries everywhere celebrate International Peace Day on the 21st of September.

Paragraph 4

Every year on September 21, students around the world participate in a project called Pinwheels for Peace. Students make their own pinwheels. They decorate them with drawings, paintings, or photographs. Some students do not have cameras, so they can't take photographs. Students also write a personal wish for peace on the inside of the pinwheel. Finally, they "plant" their pinwheels outside their schools. Then, when the wind blows, the pinwheels spin and each wish is sent out into the world.

B. Compare answers with another student. Are they the same?

CONCLUDING SENTENCES

In many paragraphs, there is a **concluding sentence**. The concluding sentence is the last sentence of the paragraph. The concluding sentence often restates the main idea of the paragraph. It can repeat words and ideas from the topic sentence. This reminds the reader about the main idea and summarizes the main idea. The concluding sentence can also give the writer's opinion or feelings about the topic.

Example:

> ***Every year on September 21, students around the world participate in a project called Pinwheels for Peace.*** *Students make their own pinwheels. They decorate them with drawings, paintings, or photographs. Students also write a personal wish for peace on the inside of the pinwheel. Finally, they "plant" their pinwheels outside their schools. Then, when the wind blows, the pinwheels spin and each wish is sent out into the world.* ***This project is a great way for students to share their ideas about peace.***

The topic sentence and the concluding sentence repeat some of the same words:

project

students

peace

The concluding sentence also gives the writer's opinion about the topic:

a great way for students to share ideas

A good concluding sentence helps your reader understand and think about the topic.

EXERCISE 7

A. *Read the paragraphs. Underline the concluding sentence. Circle the repeated words in the topic sentence and concluding sentence.*

Paragraph 1

My hometown Jamesville is a great place to live. It is clean and safe. There is not a lot of crime. There are a lot of parks and green places. There are many good restaurants and interesting small shops downtown. Best of all, Jamesville has a great school system with excellent teachers, so there are many families with young children. I am glad I live in a great place called Jamesville.

Paragraph 2

The ostrich is a special bird in several ways. First of all, it is the world's largest and heaviest bird. Secondly, ostriches cannot fly, but they can run very fast on their strong legs. In fact, ostriches can run 43 miles (70 km) per hour. The ostrich has the largest eyes of any land animal. Each eye is about 2 inches (5 cm) across. It is also the only bird with only two toes on its feet. The ostrich's egg is also the biggest egg in the world. These are some of the ways that ostriches are special.

B. *Compare answers with another student. Are they the same?*

EXERCISE 8

A. *Read the paragraphs. Choose the best concluding sentence for each paragraph. Circle the letter.*

Paragraph 1

My parents love to travel. They usually take one big trip every year. First, they decide where they want to go. Then they spend a lot of time preparing for their trip. They read books. They talk to people. On these trips, my father takes many pictures, and my mother keeps a travel journal. They write a lot of postcards. When they get home, they show us their pictures and tell us about their adventure.

a. My mother likes to write in her travel journal.
b. My parents enjoy the trips they take together.
c. I like to travel with my parents.

Paragraph 2

My father is very proud of his vegetable garden. Every year he plants tomatoes, peppers, cucumbers, peas, carrots, and onions. This year he also planted eggplants and zucchini. He works in his garden every evening and on the weekends in spring and summer. The vegetables from his garden taste better than the vegetables you buy from the supermarket.

a. It's no surprise that he is so proud of his garden.
b. My father is also a great cook.
c. The supermarkets sell fresh vegetables.

(continued)

Paragraph 3

My grandmother's ninetieth birthday was a special time for the whole family. Our whole family came to her birthday party. At the party, everyone told stories about a special time they remember with my grandmother. We had dinner and birthday cake. Then my grandmother opened her presents. My sister and I made a scrapbook for her. It had pictures of everyone in the family.

  a. My grandmother loved the scrapbook.
  b. My grandfather's birthday and my birthday are on the same day.
  c. It was a wonderful day for the whole family.

B. *Compare answers with another student. Are they the same?*

EXERCISE 9

A. *Work with a partner. Read the paragraphs. Underline the topic sentence. Write a concluding sentence.*

Paragraph 1

Music is an important part of my life. I studied the piano when I was young. Now I'm learning the guitar. I also love to sing. When I feel sad or upset, I go in my room and listen to music. Sometimes, I sing along or play the guitar with the music. It always makes me feel better. _____

_____

Paragraph 2

Alice always wanted to be a fashion designer. When she was a teenager, she read all the fashion magazines. She also read biographies of famous fashion designers and books about the fashion industry. She learned to sew. She made clothes for herself and her two sisters. _____

_____

Paragraph 3

  I like to play word games. My favorite game is called *Words with Friends*. I play this game on my smartphone. I also like to play *Hangman* and *Jumble Words*. They are both fun word games. Sometimes when I'm with my friends we play a word game called *Dictionary*. On long car rides my whole family plays two old word games called *Geography* and *Ghost*. _____

_____

 B. *With your partner, compare answers with another pair. Are they similar?*

WRITING TASK

> Write a paragraph about one of your favorite things.

 A. *Prepare for writing. Follow these steps:*

  1. Choose one of these topics.

   Your favorite:

   • season   • holiday   • place

   • animal   • food   • activity

  2. Find another student with the same topic. Take turns and ask questions about the topic.

   Examples:

   What is your favorite animal?

   Why is it your favorite?

   What is it like?

> **Note:** When you write, you need to think about your reader. What does the reader want to know about your topic? What questions will the reader have about your topic? Think about the questions. Ask yourself these questions and answer the questions in your writing.

  3. Complete this sentence. It will be the topic sentence in your paragraph.

   My favorite _____ is _____ .

(continued)

4. Write four supporting sentences. Think about your topic. Ask yourself questions. Answer the questions in your writing.

> **Remember**
>
> Supporting sentences give details, facts, and examples about the main idea in your topic sentence. Do not include irrelevant sentences. Include only sentences that support the main idea.

_____

_____

_____

_____

5. Complete one of these sentences for your concluding sentence.

- For these reasons, I _____ .
- It's no surprise that I _____ .
- I'm glad that I _____ .

B. *Write a paragraph about your favorite things. Use your sentences in Steps 3, 4, and 5.*

_____

_____

_____

_____

_____

C. *Work with a partner. Take turns. Read your paragraphs aloud.*

Check Your Writing

A. *Read your paragraph in the Writing Task. Use this form to check your paragraph.*

Paragraph Checklist

The paragraph . . .

- has a topic sentence with a clear main idea. ☐
- has supporting sentences about the main idea. ☐
- has a concluding sentence with words from the topic sentence. ☐
- has only complete sentences. ☐
- has correct paragraph format, punctuation, and capitalization. ☐
- has a correct title. ☐

B. *Correct any errors in your paragraph. Then write your paragraph again.*

Further Practice

Journal or Blog Topic

- Choose another one of the topics from the Writing Task on page 149. Write a paragraph about the topic.

Part 3, Units 1 and 2, describe basic paragraphs. A paragraph is a group of sentences about one topic. In most paragraphs, the first sentence—the topic sentence—tells the topic and the main idea about the topic. The next sentences—the supporting sentences—give more information about the main idea. The concluding sentence repeats the ideas in the topic sentence. Some writers also include an opinion about the main idea in the concluding sentence.

In this unit, you will learn about a special kind of paragraph, a listing paragraph. There are several ways to organize the information in a paragraph in English. In a listing paragraph, you organize the information in lists. Listing information in a paragraph is an effective way to organize your ideas for your reader.

Warm Up

A. ***Look at the picture. What do you see? What are the people doing? List three things.***

1. _____

2. _____

3. _____

B. *Think about your weekends. What do you like to do? List three things.*

1. _____

2. _____

3. _____

C. *Share your lists in Exercises A and B with another student. Are they similar? Talk about the things you and your partner like to do.*

LISTING PARAGRAPHS

Listing paragraphs are a very common type of paragraph in English. In a listing paragraph, you write the main idea in the topic sentence. Then, you support the main idea by listing reasons and examples.

Example:

> **Catching Up on the Weekend**
>
> There are several things I like to do on the weekend. First of all, I like to sleep late. I also like to spend time with my friends. We usually meet for lunch or go shopping. Finally, I enjoy going to the movies. I always look forward to the weekend. I can catch up on the things I don't have time to do during the week.

In this paragraph the topic is *weekend activities.*

The main idea is *things I like to do on the weekend.*

The writer lists three examples of things she likes to do on the weekend.

- Sleep late
- Spend time with friends
- Go to the movies

A. Read the paragraph. Answer the questions.

I Love Mysteries

I love to read mystery novels for several reasons. For one thing, mysteries are fun. They are like playing a game. I use the clues to try to solve the mystery, so I am never bored. In addition, mysteries are a great escape. I often forget my own problems because I am so involved in the story. Finally, I want to be a detective, so I learn a lot about crime from reading mystery novels.

1. What is the topic sentence? Underline it.
2. What is the main idea? Write it.

   _____

3. What three reasons does the writer list to support the main idea? List them.

   a. _____
   b. _____
   c. _____

B. Compare answers with another student. Are they the same?

A. Read the paragraph. Answer the questions.

Cheaper Ways to Fly

There are several ways you can save money on airline tickets. First of all, make your reservations in advance. Don't wait until the last minute. Often you can save up to 30 percent if you book your flight a month in advance. In addition, look for flights online. You can often find cheap tickets online. Check out websites like travelocity.com and cheapfares.com. Also, think about flying to a big city and then renting a car or taking a bus to get to your final destination. Flights between big cities are often cheaper than flights between smaller cities. These are just a few of the ways you can save money on your next airline ticket.

1. What is the topic sentence? Underline it.

2. What is the main idea? Write it.

_____

3. What three ways does the writer list to support the main idea? List them.

a. _____

b. _____

c. _____

B. Compare answers with another student. Are they the same?

A. *Read the paragraph. Answer the questions.*

> ### A Great Place to Go
>
> I like to go to COEX Mall in Seoul, South Korea, for several reasons. First of all, there is great food. The two international food courts offer every kind of food you can imagine. Secondly, COEX has wonderful entertainment. For example, there is a sixteen-screen cinema complex and an amazing aquarium. There is even a game room and a disco. Finally, I love to go to COEX for the fabulous shopping. There are over 250 stores. I never get tired of going to COEX Mall.

1. What is the topic sentence? Underline it.

2. What is the main idea? Write it.

   _____

3. What three reasons does the writer list to support the main idea? List them.

   a. _____

   b. _____

   c. _____

B. *Compare answers with another student. Are they the same?*

Topic Sentences for Listing Paragraphs

Like other paragraphs, listing paragraphs have a topic sentence that tells the main idea. Here are some common sentence patterns for topic sentences of listing paragraphs.

- There are several reasons I like . . .
- There are two reasons I don't . . .
- There are many ways you can . . .
- There are three things . . .
- I like _____ for several reasons.
- I love _____ for three reasons.

Read the topics. Write a topic sentence for a listing paragraph about these topics. Follow the examples in number 1.

1. shop online

   <u>There are several reasons I like to shop online.</u> **OR** <u>I like to shop</u>
   <u>online for several reasons.</u>

2. learn a new language

   _____

3. make new friends

   _____

4. eat a healthy breakfast

   _____

Using Transitions

A **transition** is a word or phrase that connects ideas. Transitions link the information in your paragraph. Transitions often go at the beginning of a sentence. They are usually followed by a comma (,).

There are many different types of transition words and phrases in English. Look at the chart of listing order transitions. These transitions order or number the list of supporting sentences for the reader.

Listing Order Transitions		
First,	In addition,	Finally,
For one thing,	Also,	Most importantly,
First of all,	Secondly,	

Note: The transition word *also* can come at the beginning of the sentence or in the middle of a sentence. When *also* comes in the middle of a sentence, do not use a comma.

Also, many people recommend this restaurant.
*The restaurant is very crowded. It is **also** very expensive.* (Use *also* after the verb *be*.)
*The restaurant looks nice. It **also** smells good.* (Use *also* before the main verb.)

A. Read the paragraphs. Underline the transitions.

Paragraph 1

There are several reasons the Comfort Hotel is losing business. First of all, the hotel is in a dangerous neighborhood. In addition, the prices at the Comfort Hotel are too high. For example, a room with one double bed costs $200 per night. Other hotels near the Comfort Hotel charge much less. Most importantly, the rooms at the Comfort Hotel are small and dirty. These are a few of the reasons the hotel is having trouble.

Paragraph 2

There are several ways you can improve your English. First, you can do crossword puzzles and other types of word games. They help you improve your vocabulary, and you have fun at the same time. Secondly, read as much as possible in English. For example, read books and articles on topics that are familiar and interesting to you. Finally, listen to speakers of English on the radio, the Internet, or TV. These are just a few of the many ways you can improve your English language skills.

B. Compare answers with another student. Are they the same?

A. Complete the paragraphs. Use order transitions.

Paragraph 1

Online dictionaries have several advantages. _____ online dictionaries are always up to date. New words can be added to an online dictionary easily. _____ online dictionaries are fast and easy to use. You just type in the word you are looking for and press enter and the definition appears in a few seconds. _____ you can hear how the word is pronounced. All you have to do is press the audio icon. More and more people are using online dictionaries because of all of their advantages.

Paragraph 2

I like to ride my bike to school for several reasons. _____, it's good exercise. My apartment is 2 miles from campus, so I get a good workout riding to and from school. _____ I don't have to look for a parking spot. There aren't enough parking lots around campus, and it takes a long time or a lot of luck to find a place to park. _____, riding a bike is good for the environment. Bicycles don't use gas or pollute the air. I'm glad I decided to buy a bike and ride to school.

Paragraph 3

There are several reasons people think Switzerland is a wonderful place to live. _____, Swiss cities are safe and clean. The crime rate is low, and the streets and parks are never dirty. _____, Switzerland is a healthy place to live. There is very little pollution, and the health care system is excellent. _____ Switzerland's natural beauty makes it a great place to live. For example, you can see the beautiful snow-covered Alps from almost any place in Switzerland. There are lovely lakes and green meadows. Living in Switzerland is like living in a postcard.

B. Compare answers with another student. Are they the same?

A. *Read the two topic sentences. Find sentences to suppport each one. Label the supporting sentences "1" or "2."*

Topic Sentences

1. I like to shop online for several reasons.

2. I do not like to shop online for several reasons.

Supporting Sentences

___2___ **a.** Online shopping is too impersonal because there isn't a salesperson to help.

___1___ **b.** Online shopping is convenient, and I can shop from the comfort of my home.

_____ **c.** I can't try things on or see the actual items.

_____ **d.** I can shop anytime I want.

_____ **e.** I like to pay for my purchases in cash, but I can't do that on the Internet.

_____ **f.** When I shop online, I don't have to wait in lines to pay for my purchases.

_____ **g.** It is easy to compare many products quickly on the Internet.

_____ **h.** I don't like waiting for my purchases to arrive in the mail.

B. *Choose one of the topic sentences in Exercise A. Write a paragraph with the topic sentence and supporting sentences. Write it on a separate piece of paper. Include transitions.*

Remember

A paragraph in English has a special format. When you write a paragraph, you need to think about the way it looks and follow paragraph format guidelines.

(See Part 3, Unit 1, for more information on paragraph format.)

C. *Compare paragraphs in a small group. Are they similar?*

A. *Read the list of qualities of a good friend. Write the name of someone you know who has each quality. You can write the name of different people or the same person.*

1. kind _____
2. funny _____
3. smart _____
4. helpful _____
5. sincere _____

6. good listener _____
7. reliable _____
8. honest _____
9. fun _____
10. generous _____

B. *Work in a small group. Follow these steps to write a paragraph.*

1. Discuss the qualities and the people in your list in Exercise A. Explain why you chose each person.

2. What are the three most important qualities of a good friend?

   a. _____

   b. _____

   c. _____

3. Write a listing paragraph together about the most important qualities. Use transitions to help your reader understand your ideas. Begin your paragraph: *There are three important qualities of a good friend.*

4. Choose one person in your group to read the paragraph to the class.

Using Examples

Examples can help explain your ideas. They are a good way to support your ideas in a paragraph. Listing paragraphs often include examples. The example makes the item clear.

It is helpful to tell your reader that you are giving an example. One way is to introduce the example. Some common phrases to introduce examples are:

For example,   *For instance,*

Note: A complete sentence follows the phrases *For example* or *For instance.* Use a comma after these phrases. A complete sentence has a subject and a verb.

Examples:

$\overset{\text{Sub.}}{} \overset{\text{Verb}}{}$

Carl is an excellent musician. **For example,** *he plays the guitar, the piano, and the trumpet very well.*

There are many things you can do with young children on a rainy day. **For instance,**
$\overset{\text{Sub.}}{} \overset{\text{Verb}}{}$
you can play board games, bake cookies, or do art projects.

EXERCISE 9

Work with a partner. Read the paragraph. Underline the example sentences. Then answer the questions.

A Wonderful Roommate

There are several reasons why Claire is a wonderful college roommate. First of all, she is very considerate. For example, she doesn't talk on her phone when I am studying. When her phone rings, she goes in the hall to talk. In addition, Claire is very helpful. For instance, last week she helped me clean the room and get ready for a visit from my parents. Most importantly, Claire is really friendly. All my friends enjoy spending time with us in our room. I am so lucky to have Claire for a roommate.

1. What is the topic sentence? _____

2. What three reasons does the writer give to support her main idea?

_____

_____

_____

3. What example does the writer use to explain her first reason?

_____

4. What example does the writer use to explain her second reason?

_____

5. What detail does the writer use to explain her third reason?

_____

6. What is the concluding sentence? _____

Work with a partner. Read the paragraph. Underline the example sentences. Then answer the questions.

Helping the Environment

There are many ways you can help the environment. For one thing, you can recycle. For example, you can return empty glass, paper, and plastic containers to special recycling centers. You can also save energy in your home. For instance, you can use less hot water and turn the lights off when you leave a room. Finally, you can help the environment by planting a tree. Trees are good for the air and the land. These are just a few of the many ways you can "go green."

1. What is the topic sentence? _____

2. What three ways does the writer give to support the main idea?

_____

_____

_____

3. What example does the writer use to explain the first way?

_____

4. What example does the writer use to explain the second way?

_____

5. What detail does the writer use to explain the third way?

_____

6. What is the concluding sentence? _____

A. *Read the sentences and examples. Write the sentences again. Introduce the examples.*

1. Sentence: My family always spends time together on the weekends.
   Example: I cook a big family dinner, and we all eat together.

   My family always spends time together on the weekends. For example, I cook a big family dinner, and we all eat together.

2. Sentence: I like to teach my children about gardening.
   Example: I encourage them to help me plant vegetables.

   _____

   _____

3. Sentence: I enjoy reading on the weekends.
   Example: I catch up on the news of the week and read interesting articles in the paper.

   _____

   _____

4. Sentence: I like to spend time outdoors on the weekends.
   Example: I go hiking or bike riding almost every Saturday.

   _____

   _____

5. Sentence: I try to live a healthy lifestyle.
   Example: I go to the gym three times a week.

   _____

   _____

B. *Compare answers with another student. Are they the same?*

A. Work with a partner. Complete the sentences.

1. Watching too much TV is not good for children for several reasons.

   First of all, _____.

   For example, _____.

2. Several kinds of music can be relaxing. First, _____

   _____.

   For example, _____.

3. There are many ways to eat in a healthy way. First, _____

   _____.

   For instance, _____.

4. There are several things I like to do on the weekends. For one thing,

   _____.

   For instance, _____.

B. Compare answers with another pair. Are they similar?

A. Work in a small group. Answer these questions.

1. Read the paragraph in Exercise 2A on page 155 again. Where can you add *For example* and *For instance*? Add them to the paragraph.

2. Read the paragraph in Exercise 3A on page 156 again. Find the phrase *For example* and circle it. Where can you add *For instance* in this paragraph? Add it to the paragraph.

3. Read Paragraph 1 in Exercise 5 on page 158 again. Find the phrase *For example* and circle it. Where can you introduce another example? Add another example to the paragraph. Begin with *For instance*.

B. Compare answers with another group. Are they the same?

WRITING TASK

Write a paragraph about your hometown.

A. *Prepare for writing. Follow these steps:*

1. Work with a partner. Describe your hometown to your partner. Explain why your hometown is or is not a good place to visit.

2. Choose one of these topic sentences:

   My hometown is a good place to visit for several reasons.

   My hometown is not a good place to visit for several reasons.

3. Write your topic sentence. Make a list of reasons to support your topic sentence. Include an example to support each of your reasons.

   Topic sentence: _____

   Reason # 1: _____

   Example: _____

   Reason # 2: _____

   Example: _____

   Reason # 3: _____

   Example: _____

B. *Write your listing paragraph on a separate piece of paper. Use your reasons and examples from Step 3. Include transitions. Write a title.*

> ### Remember
>
> A paragraph in English has a special format. When you write a paragraph, you need to think about the way it looks and follow paragraph format guidelines.
>
> *(See Part 3, Unit 1, for more information on paragraph format.)*

Check Your Writing

A. *Read your paragraph in the Writing Task. Use this form to check your writing.*

Listing Paragraph Checklist

The paragraph . . .

- has a topic sentence with a clear main idea. ☐
- has supporting sentences about the main idea. ☐
- lists reasons and examples that explain the main idea. ☐
- uses transitions to help the reader follow the ideas. ☐
- has a concluding sentence. ☐
- has only complete sentences. ☐
- has correct paragraph format, punctuation, and capitalization. ☐
- has a correct title. ☐

B. *Correct any errors in your paragraph. Then write your paragraph again.*

Further Practice

Journal or Blog Topic

- Choose a building or tourist site in your hometown. Think about these questions. Make a list of your ideas.
  - Why is it a good place to visit?
  - What can you do there?
- Use your list. Write a listing paragraph about a building or tourist site in your hometown.

Writing Instructions

Have you ever tried to teach someone a game? Sometimes even simple games are difficult to teach. You usually begin with the first step in the game and continue until the last step. Some paragraphs include instructions on how to do things. These paragraphs give the instructions the same way you teach a game, that is, in a set order. They usually include words that help order the steps. The topic sentence introduces what the paragraph teaches. The supporting sentences list the steps in order. The concluding sentence often gives an opinion about the instructions and repeats information from the topic sentence. In this unit, you will learn about writing **instruction paragraphs**.

Warm Up

Look at the picture. Discuss the questions in a small group.

- What is the man doing?
- Do you usually read the instructions before you make something?
- What makes some instructions better than others?
- How are most instructions organized?

USING TIME ORDER TO WRITE INSTRUCTIONS

Time order is a way to organize the supporting sentences in your paragraph. When you use time order to give instructions, you explain the first step, then the second step, then the third step, and so on. Organizing an instruction paragraph with time order will help your reader follow the steps in your instructions.

EXERCISE 1

A. Look at the pictures. They teach the steps in the game Tic-Tac-Toe.

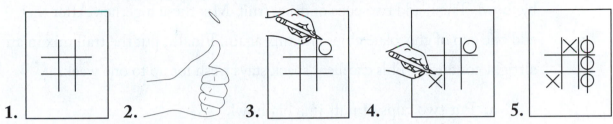

1.   2.   3.   4.   5.

B. Work with a partner. Put the steps in order. Write the number of the picture beside the correct instruction. Follow the example.

_____ Next, flip a coin. The person with "heads" plays first.

_____ Then, the next person writes an X in one of the boxes.

_____ Finally, take turns. Write your X or O in the empty boxes. Try to be the first person with your three X's or three O's in a row. You win!

_____ The first person writes an O in one of the boxes.

_1_ First, draw a Tic-Tac-Toe board. It looks like a large number symbol (#). It has nine boxes.

C. Follow the instructions and play Tic-Tac-Toe.

D. Read the example paragraph a student wrote about how to play Tic-Tac-Toe.

> *Tic-Tac-Toe is an easy and fun game. All you need is a pencil or pen, and a piece of paper. First, draw a Tic-Tac-Toe board. It looks like a large number symbol (#). It has nine boxes. Next, flip a coin. The person with "heads" plays first. The first person writes an "O" in one of the boxes. Then, the next person writes an "X" in one of the boxes. Finally, take turns. Write your X or O in the empty boxes. Try to be the first person with your three X's or three O's in a row. You win!*

In this paragraph the topic is *Tic-Tac-Toe*. The main idea is *an easy and fun game*. The author writes the steps of the game in order. You move from one step to the next. This is time order.

Read the instructions in the paragraph. Then put the steps in order.

Here is a recipe for trail mix, an easy and healthy snack. First of all, get everything together. You need two kinds of nuts. For example, you can use almonds, cashews, or peanuts. Then, you need two kinds of dried fruits. For instance, you can use raisins, pineapple, or bananas. You also need something sweet. Chocolate chips are a good choice. Next, put two cups of nuts in a big bowl. Then, add two cups of dried fruit. Mix these together. After that, add one cup of chocolate chips and mix again. Finally, put the trail mix in an airtight container. This excellent snack stays fresh for up to one week.

_____ **a.** Put two cups of nuts in a big bowl.

__1__ **b.** Get everything together.

_____ **c.** Add two cups of dried fruit.

_____ **d.** Put the trail mix in an airtight container.

_____ **e.** Mix these together.

_____ **f.** Add one cup of chocolate chips and mix again.

EXERCISE 3

A. **Read the instructions in the paragraph. Then answer the questions.**

A banana smoothie is a simple and delicious treat. Here is a recipe for banana smoothies. First, put a frozen banana, half a cup of yogurt, and half a cup of fresh orange juice in a blender. Next, blend it for one minute. Then add a quarter of a cup of fresh blueberries. Blend everything for another fifteen seconds. Finally, pour your smoothie in a glass. Enjoy this refreshing fruit treat!

1. How many steps are there in these instructions? _____

2. What are the steps? List the steps in order on a separate piece of paper.

B. **Compare answers with another student. Are they the same?**

Writing Topic Sentences for Instruction Paragraphs

Instruction paragraphs begin with a *topic sentence* that tells the reader you are going to explain a step-by-step process. The *topic* of the sentence is the process you describe in the paragraph.

Topic sentences of instruction paragraphs often begin like this:

- You can . . . if you follow this recipe.

  You can make a delicious cake if you follow this recipe. (Topic: how to make a delicious cake)

- Here is an easy way to (a recipe for) . . .

  Here is an easy way to make a birthday card. (Topic: how to make a birthday card)

  Here is an easy recipe for trail mix, a healthy snack. (Topic: how to make trail mix)

- It is easy to (not hard to) . . .

  It is easy to play checkers. (Topic: how to play checkers)

  It is not hard to learn how to park a car. (Topic: how to park a car)

EXERCISE 4

Work with a partner. Write a topic sentence for an instruction paragraph about these topics.

1. how to make a cheese omelette

   _____

2. how to plan a party

   _____

3. how to paint a room

   _____

4. how to play tag

   _____

5. how to apply for a student visa

   _____

6. how to open a bank account

   _____

Time Order Transitions

Part 3, Unit 3, introduces transitions of order or number in listing paragraphs. In an instruction paragraph, writers often use transitions, too. These transitions tell **time order**. They order the steps in the instructions for the reader. Transitions often come at the beginning of a sentence. They usually have a comma (,) after them. Here are a few time order transitions you can use in your writing.

Time Order Transitions for an Instruction Paragraph		
First,	Second,	After that,
First of all,	Next,	Finally,
	Then,	Lastly,

EXERCISE 5

A. *Read the paragraphs in Exercises 2 and 3A on page 170 again. Underline the transitions in the paragraphs.*

B. *Compare answers with another student. Are they the same?*

EXERCISE 6

A. *Read the paragraph. Underline the transitions.*

Here is an easy way to make window cleaner. First of all, get everything together. You need liquid detergent, vinegar, water, and a spray bottle. Then, pour a half a teaspoon of liquid detergent, three tablespoons of vinegar, and two cups of water into your spray bottle. Finally, shake the bottle a few times, and your window cleaner is ready. It is cheap and easy. Unfortunately, you still need to clean your windows!

B. *Compare answers with a partner. Are they the same?*

A. *Complete the paragraphs. Use time order transitions.*

Paragraph 1

Here is a simple exercise to help you relax. _____, sit on the floor and cross your legs. _____, close your eyes. _____, breathe in slowly and count to four. Hold your breath and count to four. Breathe out slowly and count to four. Continue this exercise for several minutes. _____, open your eyes. See how relaxed you are.

Paragraph 2

A Waldorf salad is a delicious and impressive dish. Just follow these five simple steps. _____, chop two apples, a cup of walnuts, and a cup of celery. _____, mix them together in a large bowl. _____, add a cup of sliced grapes, a cup of yogurt or mayonnaise, and two tablespoons of lemon juice. Carefully stir all the ingredients together. _____, add salt and pepper to taste. Now you are ready to serve and enjoy your salad.

Paragraph 3

Here is an easy way to cut flowers from your garden. _____, you should cut the flowers early in the morning. As soon as you cut each stem put it in a pail of cool water. When you have enough flowers, bring them inside. _____, remove the bottom leaves and recut the stems at a diagonal. _____ arrange the cut flowers in a pretty vase with fresh water.

B. *Compare answers with a partner. Are they the same?*

Imperative Sentences

We often use **imperative sentences** when we give instructions. Imperative sentences are different from other sentences. Unlike other sentences, we do not write the subject in imperative sentences. The subject is always *you,* but we do not include it in the sentence. When we write imperative sentences, we always use the simple form (the base form) of the verb.

Examples:

Close your eyes.   Continue this exercise.

We use *do not* (or *don't*) to make negative imperative sentences.

Examples:

Do not add a lot of salt.   Don't stir the ingredients together.

EXERCISE 8

A. Read the paragraph in Exercise 6 on page 172 again. Circle the imperative verbs in the paragraph.

B. Compare answers with another student. Are they the same?

EXERCISE 9

A. Read Paragraph 1 in Exercise 7A again on page 173. How many imperative verbs are there? _____

B. List the imperative verbs in Exercise 7A on a separate sheet of paper.

C. Compare answers with another student. Are they the same?

EXERCISE 10

A. Work in a group. Read this paragraph. Correct the imperative verbs. There are five mistakes.

Here is an easy way to make a copy of your work. First, find a copy machine. Next, lifting the top of the copy machine and put your work on the glass. Then, closes the top and selects the number of copies. Pushing the copy button and waiting for your copy. This is a fast and easy way to make copies.

B. Write the correct paragraph on a separate piece of paper.

Match the imperative verbs in column A with the correct phrase in column B. Then write the imperative sentence on a separate piece of paper. Follow the example.

A	B
1. vacuum	____ **a.** your clothes
2. fold	____ **b.** your bed
3. throw	____ **c.** the floor
4. sweep	_1_ **d.** the rug
5. make	____ **e.** your shoes in the closet
6. put	____ **f.** the trash away

Example:

Vacuum the rug.

Commas in a Series

The **comma** (,) is an important punctuation mark in written English. It is like a pause in speaking. In a list of items, commas separate the items. The items can be single words or phrases. We use commas to separate three or more items in a list. We often add "*and*" before the last item in the list. We use "*or*" before the last item when there is a choice.

Examples:

You need some liquid detergent, vinegar, water, and a spray bottle.
You can use almonds, cashews, or peanuts.

Note: We do not use a comma when there are only two items, for example, *Mix oil and vinegar in a bowl.*

A. Add commas to these lists where necessary. Follow the example in number 1.

1. Put the vinegar, olive oil, and onions in a bowl.
2. You need two pieces of bread and a half a cup of milk.
3. Then, mix the tomatoes corn salt and pepper.
4. Add the onions and carrots to the soup.
5. Slowly stir the sugar vanilla and melted butter.
6. Melt the chocolate and butter in a small pan.
7. You need some glue two pieces of paper and a pair of scissors.
8. Find some paper a marker glue and cotton balls.

B. Compare answers with another student. Are they the same?

WRITING TASK

Write a paragraph that gives instructions.

A. Prepare for writing. Follow these steps:

1. Work with a partner. Read the list of topics. Choose one and explain to your partner how to do or make it. (Or you may choose another topic that you know how to do or make well.)

   • How to make a call on your cell phone.
   • How to send a text message
   • How to make a glass of iced tea
   • How to make an e-card
   • How to plan a party
   • How to make your favorite food
   • How to play a game

2. Choose a topic for your paragraph and write a topic sentence.

   Topic Sentence: _____

3. Make a list of steps for your instructions. Put the steps in time order.

_____

_____

_____

_____

_____

B. *Write your instruction paragraph on a separate piece of paper. Use your topic sentence and the steps in Exercise A. Include at least three time order transitions. Use imperative sentences.*

Remember

A paragraph in English has a special format. When you write a paragraph, you need to think about the way it looks and follow paragraph format guidelines.

(See Part 3, Unit 1, for more information about paragraph format.)

Check Your Writing

A. *Read your paragraph in the Writing Task. Use this form to check your paragraph.*

Instruction Paragraph Checklist

The paragraph . . .

- has a correct title. ☐
- has a topic sentence that introduces the item. ☐
- has supporting sentences about the item. ☐
- has steps in the correct order. ☐
- includes at least three time order transitions. ☐
- uses imperative sentences correctly. ☐
- has a concluding sentence that gives an opinion about the instructions. ☐
- has correct paragraph format, punctuation, and capitalization. ☐

B. *Correct any errors in your paragraph. Then write your paragraph again.*

Further Practice

Project Idea

Make a class cookbook. Follow these steps:

1. Choose a topic:
   - Your favorite dish
   - A popular dish from your country
   - A family recipe
2. Write the instructions for this dish.
3. Include a photo of the dish, if possible.
4. Make copies of your instructions for everyone in your class.
5. Put all the recipes together in a class cookbook.
6. Design a cover for the cookbook.

Vocabulary Building

Vocabulary Building Strategies

Good vocabulary is an important part of writing. Using the correct words makes your ideas clear and helps your reader understand your writing more easily. Learning the meaning of a new word may be easy, but remembering it is more difficult. Vocabulary strategies are ways to help you learn and remember new words.

In this unit, you will learn several strategies. Try them and see which ones work best for you.

- Read as much as you can in English.
- Keep a vocabulary notebook.
- Make vocabulary flash cards.
- Review and practice new words often.

Warm Up

A. ***What do you do when you see or hear a new word? Check (✓) the statements that are true for you.***

- ☐ I try to guess the meaning of the word.
- ☐ I look up the word in an English-English dictionary.
- ☐ I ask the teacher or a classmate for the meaning of the word.
- ☐ I look up the word in a bilingual dictionary.
- ☐ I look up the word in an online or electronic dictionary.
- ☐ I ignore the word.

B. ***Compare answers with the class.***

STRATEGY 1: READ! READ! READ!

You can build your vocabulary by reading a lot. Reading introduces you to many new words. Sometimes, you can guess the meaning of the words from hints in the reading. (Hints are often other words or information in the sentence.) Other times, you may need to look the word up in a dictionary. Often you will see the same word in different types of reading. The more times you see a word, the better you will remember it.

EXERCISE 1

A. Read the passages.

> My older sister Vicky is an amazing person. She is very popular at school. All of her teachers and classmates like her a lot. She's a good friend and a great sister. She is also a great dancer. She takes dance lessons every week, and she practices every day. Everyone likes to watch Vicky dance. She plans to major in dance at college. Then she wants to move to New York and become a professional dancer. I know she will be very successful. As you can see, I'm a big fan of my big sister!

Soccer

Soccer is the most popular sport in the world. Over 3.5 billion people around the world are soccer fans. People in almost every country like to play or watch soccer. Many children dream about becoming professional soccer players. But it isn't easy. It takes a lot of skill, training, and hard work to become a professional player. Many people think the best soccer player of all time is Brazil's Pelé. Other famous professional soccer players are David Beckham (England), Franz Beckenbauer (Germany), and Diego Maradona (Argentina).

(continued)

Wendy's Weekly Blog

I love the TV reality show *MasterChef* because I want to be a professional chef some day. I watch a lot of cooking shows, but *MasterChef* is my favorite. It's the most popular cooking show on TV. Millions of fans all over the world watch *MasterChef*. The star of the show is a Scottish chef named Gordon Ramsey. One day I hope to become like Gordon. I just bought the *MasterChef* cookbook. Has anyone read it yet? Let me know which recipes you like. I made the Vietnamese chicken and rice with cabbage salad. It was DELICIOUS!

B. *Find and underline these words in each of the passages in Exercise A.*

| popular | watch | professional | fan(s) |

C. *Guess the meanings of these words. Write your meanings on the lines. Use hints from the passages to help you. Write the hints you used. Follow the example.*

popular: liked by many people

Hints: Everyone likes her. Over 3.5 billion people are soccer fans.
Millions of fans watch MasterChef.

watch: _____

Hints: _____

_____

professional: _____

Hints: _____

_____

fan: _____

Hints: _____

_____

D. *Compare guesses with another student. Are they similar?*

A.   *Read the passage and underline words you do not know.*

Raksha Bandhan is a special festival. Brothers and sisters in northern India celebrate Raksha Bandhan every August. They celebrate this festival to show their love for each other. Girls tie a bracelet around their brothers' wrists. The bracelet is made of silk threads. It is called a rakhi. Then the boys make a promise to their sisters. They promise to protect their sisters. The siblings also exchange gifts. The tradition of celebrating Raksha Bandhan is very old. People in India celebrated Raksha Bandhan over 500 years ago.

B.   *Look up three of the words you do not know in a dictionary. Write the words and the definitions.*

   1. Word: _____

   Definition: _____

   2. Word: _____

   Definition: _____

   3. Word: _____

   Definition: _____

C.   *Share your words and definitions with another student. Are they the same?*

   (See Part 4, Unit 2, for more on using a dictionary.)

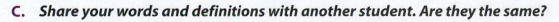

STRATEGY 2: KEEP A VOCABULARY NOTEBOOK

A **vocabulary notebook** is a notebook you use only for new words. Write new words in your notebook every day, study them often, and use them in your writing.

What Words Should You Include in Your Notebook?

Many English words may be new for you. How do you know which words to put in your vocabulary notebook? Here are two kinds of words you can include:

- Words you see more than one time
- Words you see in a few different places

What Information Should You Include About Each Word?

Include information about each word that will help you remember the meaning. Of course, you should include the spelling, definition, and part of speech. It is also helpful to write the sentence where you found the word. You might include different kinds of information for different kinds of words. For example, you can include the past tense of irregular verbs. You can also draw a simple picture, write the word in your language, and include synonyms and antonyms.

EXERCISE 3

A. Read the example from a student's vocabulary notebook. Check (✓) the information in the example.

WORD	DEFINITION	OTHER INFORMATION
Traffic (Noun) "There wasn't much <u>traffic</u> on the road."	The vehicles (cars, buses, trucks) moving along a road or street	**traffic jam** (long line of vehicles that are not moving) **traffic light** (red, yellow, green; Colored light that shows if you should stop or go) **heavy traffic** (a lot of traffic)

☑ the new word　　　　　　　　　　☐ a picture of the word
☐ a translation from the student's language　☐ common phrases that use the word
☐ a dictionary definition　　　　　　☐ the part of speech
☐ a sentence with the word　　　　　☐ a synonym or antonym

B. *Work with your class. Answer these questions and make a list.*

- What other information will help you learn new words?
- What other information do you want in your vocabulary notebook?

_____

_____

_____

_____

EXERCISE 4

A. *Look in Part 3. Read some of the paragraphs in Units 1, 2, 3, or 4. Find three new words. Write information to help you remember each word.*

Word	Definition	Other Information

Word	Definition	Other Information

Word	Definition	Other Information

B. *Compare words with another student. Did you choose any of the same words?*

Organizing a Vocabulary Notebook

There are several ways to organize the words in your vocabulary notebook. Choose the way that works best for you. One way to organize your words is in alphabetical order (a, b, c, d . . .).

You can also organize the words into groups (or categories) according to topics. For example, you could have topics like these.

- Family
- Weather
- Sports
- Jobs
- Travel

EXERCISE 5

A. *Work with a partner. Complete the chart. Write words from the box in the correct category. Use a dictionary, if necessary.*

aunt	cloudy	jacket	sibling
blouse	cousin	mechanic	skirt
chef	dentist	nephew	snowy
chilly	humid	reporter	vest

Family	Weather	Jobs	Clothes
aunt			

B. *Read the paragraph. Find two more words from each category in Exercise A. Write them in the chart.*

My uncle Frank is a lawyer. He works at a small law office in Portland, Oregon. He wears a suit and tie at work. His wife, Julie, is a judge. She wears a long, black robe in court. Frank and Julie met in law school and got married twenty years ago. They have busy lives, but they take a vacation every year. They like to go to sunny and warm places. Last year they went to Hawaii.

C. *Work with a partner. Make a list. What other ways can you organize words in a vocabulary notebook?*

- _____
- _____
- _____
- _____

D. *How do you want to organize your vocabulary notebook? Write your answer.*

_____

EXERCISE 6

A. *Start a vocabulary notebook. Choose five new words. You can choose words from the paragraphs in this unit or from other places.*

B. *Write the words in your notebook. Write the definition and the sentence where you found the word. Include other information that will help you remember the new word.*

C. *Work in a small group. Talk about the words you wrote in your vocabulary notebook.*

STRATEGY 3: MAKE FLASH CARDS

Flash cards are another helpful way to remember new words. It's easy to make your own flash cards with small index cards. Make flash cards for words that are difficult to remember.

Follow these steps to make flash cards:

1. Write a word you want to learn on one side.
2. Put the part of speech next to the word.
3. Write a sentence that uses the word under the word.
4. Write the definition of the word on the other side.
5. Write the word in your language under the definition.

Example:

Front

Receptionist (Noun)

Maria is the <u>receptionist</u> at a doctor's office.

Back

Someone whose job is to answer the phone and welcome people when they arrive at an office or hotel.

el recepcionista (in Spanish)

Put your cards in an envelope. Write "Words I Am Learning" on the envelope. Carry your cards with you. Study them in your free time. The more often you use your flash cards, the more you will remember the new vocabulary words.

EXERCISE 7

A. *Choose five words. Make flash cards for the words.*

B. *Put the cards in an envelope. Write "Words I Am Learning" on the envelope.*

C. *Compare cards with another student. Are they similar?*

Using Flash Cards by Yourself

Follow these steps to test yourself with your flash cards:

1. Look at the word on the front of the card. Do you know what it means?
2. Think of the definition of the word.
3. Turn the card over. Check the definition. Was your definition correct?

OR

1. Read the definition on the back of the card. Do you know what the word is?
2. Think of the word. Spell it to yourself.
3. Turn the card over. Did you know the word? Did you spell it correctly?

Put the cards with words and definitions you know well in a separate envelope. Write "Words I Know" on that envelope. When all of your cards are in that envelope, it's time to make some new cards!

Using Flash Cards with a Partner

It's helpful to review your cards with a friend or family member. Follow these steps:

1. Find a partner. Give your partner your "Words I Am Learning" envelope.
2. Your partner can ask you the words or the definitions on your cards.
3. Your partner will make sure you can say and spell the word correctly.
4. Your partner will make sure you know the definition.

EXERCISE 8

A. *Use the flash cards you made to test yourself. Follow the steps above.*

B. *Put the words you know well in another envelope. Write "Words I Know" on that envelope.*

C. *Work with another student. Review your cards with your partner. Follow the steps above.*

STRATEGY 4: PRACTICE, REVIEW, REPEAT, REINFORCE

In order to learn new words well, you need to study them often. Practice using new words. Here are some ways you can practice new words every day.

- Write them down.
- Say them out loud.
- Write sentences using the words.
- Use the words in a conversation.
- Talk about new words with classmates and friends.
- Go online and do a search of the new words.
- Get examples of the words in conversation and in writing. Use the words in different ways.

Review your vocabulary notebook and flash cards often. Make learning new words part of your daily life. Some people have a certain time every day to review vocabulary words. Other people review their words whenever they have some free time during the day.

EXERCISE 9

A. *Work with a partner. When and where can you study flash cards? Make a list.*

- _Waiting in line at a store_
- _____
- _____
- _____
- _____

B. *With your partner, join another pair. Are your ideas similar?*

EXERCISE 10

A. *Choose three words from your vocabulary notebook or flash cards.*

B. *Write a sentence for each word you chose. Underline the new word in each sentence.*

1. _____
2. _____
3. _____

C. *Wait a few days. Write a journal entry or blog post using the same three words. Underline the new words.*

D. *Wait a week. Write a paragraph using the three words you chose. Show your paragraph to your teacher. Did you use the words correctly?*

EXERCISE 11

Work with a partner. Teach your partner five new words. Follow these steps:

1. Choose five new words from a unit in *Writing Power 1*.
2. Make flash cards for the words.
3. Explain the meaning of the words.
4. Share other information about the words (for example, parts of speech or different meanings).
5. Show your partner an example sentence for each word.
6. Ask your partner to write another example sentence for each word.
7. Tell your partner to add the words to a vocabulary notebook.

Further Practice

Project Idea

- Create a vocabulary test.
  - Write five new words at the top of a blank page.
  - Write a sentence for each word. Put a blank line in place of the word.
  - Give the sentences to your partner.
  - Ask your partner to complete the sentences with the correct words.
  - Check your partner's answers.
  - Did you teach your partner well? Did your partner learn the words?
  - How many words did your partner remember?

  Example:

  > thief   garden   modern   search   coin
  > 1. I planted flowers and vegetables in
  >   my _____.

Dictionary Skills

Unit 1 of Part 4 describes several strategies for learning new words. In this unit, you will look at another important strategy: using a dictionary. A good dictionary is a valuable tool. It gives you a lot of information in one place and in an organized way. Use a dictionary often. It will help you understand and learn new words. It will also help you use words correctly.

An English learner's dictionary, such as the *Longman Study Dictionary*, is a good choice for this level. A learner's dictionary gives clear definitions. It is easy to understand. It gives additional information about the words. It shows you how to use the words. And it gives example sentences.

You can also use a bilingual dictionary in your language. Bilingual dictionaries are useful, but a learner's dictionary usually gives more information about each word.

In this unit, you will look at ways of using a dictionary and the type of information you can find in it.

Warm Up

A. *Work in a small group. Discuss the kinds of information you can find in a dictionary. Make a list. Use your own dictionary or this dictionary sample for ideas.*

1. _____ .
2. _____
3. _____
4. _____
5. _____
6. _____

B. *Join another group. Compare your lists. Which items on the list are the same? Which are different?*

---

crack¹ /kræk/ *verb*
to break or damage something so that it has a line on its surface: *I dropped my favorite coffee mug and cracked it.* | *The ice started to crack as soon as I stepped on it.*
—**cracked** *adjective* something that is cracked has a thin line in it where it has broken: *a cracked mirror*
→ see Thesaurus box at **break¹**
PHRASAL VERBS
crack down = to start dealing with a type of crime or problem more severely: *Police are cracking down on drunk drivers and making lots of arrests.*
crack someone up (*informal*) = to make someone laugh a lot: *She tells me the funniest stories. She cracks me up.*

crack² *noun*
1 a thin line where something is broken: *There were several small cracks in the vase.*
2 a very narrow space between two things or two parts of something: *The letter had fallen through a crack between the floorboards.* SYNONYM: **gap**
3 a sudden short loud noise: *I heard the crack of the bat as the hitter connected with the ball.*
4 **take a crack at (doing) something** (*informal*) = to try to do something: *I thought I'd take a crack at writing some songs.*

C. Complete the questionnaire. Check (✓) your answers. Then discuss your answers with your class.

New Words in English	Usually	Sometimes	Never
1. I look up unfamiliar words in the dictionary when I am reading.			
2. I look up unfamiliar words that I hear.			
3. I use a bilingual dictionary.			
4. I use an English-only dictionary.			
5. I look up words in an online dictionary.			
6. I look up words when I write.			

USING A DICTIONARY

A **dictionary** is very easy to use. It lists words in alphabetical order. Alphabetical order is the order of the letters of the alphabet (*a, b, c, d . . .*). The word can have a capital letter (*English*). It can be a compound word (*ice cream*). It can have an apostrophe (*o'clock*). Or it can be an abbreviation (*Mrs.*). It will not change the alphabetical order of the words in a dictionary.

> **Example:**
> Alphabetical order:
> *alphabet*
> *English*
> *ice cream*
> *Mrs.*
> *o'clock*

Looking Up Words

Look at the first few letters of a word. Many words start with the same letter. In that case, you need to look at the alphabetical order of the next letter or letters in the word. Follow the steps on the next page.

1. Sometimes the first letter of the words is the same. In this case, look at the second letter in the word for alphabetical order.

   Example:

   candy

   certain

   cover

   cream

2. Sometimes the first and second letters of the words are the same. In this case, look at the third letter in the word for alphabetical order.

   Example:

   sugar

   suit

   summer

   supper

EXERCISE 1

A. Number the words in each group in alphabetical order. Then write them in alphabetical order. Follow the example.

Group 1	Group 2
____ light	____ read
____ heavy	____ Dr.
_1_ apple	____ heroic
____ border	____ bell
____ hold	____ finish

Group 1

apple

_____

_____

_____

_____

Group 2

_____

_____

_____

_____

_____

B. *Number the words in each group in alphabetical order. Then write them in alphabetical order.*

Group 3	Group 4	Group 5
____ conquer	____ heal	____ o'clock
____ captain	____ head	____ octagon
____ clutch	____ hawk	____ October
____ crown	____ health food	____ odd jobs
____ cheat	____ hilly	____ ocean

Group 3   **Group 4**   **Group 5**

_____   _____   _____

_____   _____   _____

_____   _____   _____

_____   _____   _____

_____   _____   _____

C. *Compare answers in Exercises A and B with another student. Are they the same?*

Parts of Speech

We group words into parts of speech. The major groups (parts of speech) are nouns, verbs, adjectives, and adverbs. Other parts of speech are conjunctions, articles, and prepositions. The part of speech of a word tells you how to use it in a sentence.

The wrong part of speech makes your sentence incorrect.

Examples:

Incorrect: *She spoke soft.* (Use the adverb *softly* to describe the verb *spoke*.)
Correct: *She spoke **softly**.*

Incorrect: *I like a softly pillow.* (Use the adjective *soft* to describe the noun *pillow*.)
Correct: *I like a **soft** pillow.*

A dictionary tells you the part of speech of every word. Sometimes a word can be more than one part of speech. For example, the word *hand* can be a noun or a verb. Look up *hand* in a dictionary. You will see the two different parts of speech and two definitions for *hand*.

Examples:

*I raise my **hand** when I know the answer.* (noun)

*Can you **hand** me the dictionary?* (verb)

EXERCISE 2

A. **Read the information in the chart. Complete the chart. Write the use of each part of speech. Use your dictionary to help you. Follow the examples.**

Part of Speech	Use	Examples
Adjective (adj)	*A word that describes a noun*	She wore a **pretty** dress. He is **tired** and **hungry**.
Adverb (adv)	*A word that describes a verb, an adjective, or another adverb*	She walked **slowly** and **carefully**. He dialed the number **again**.
Conjunction (conj)	*A word that connects other words, phrases, or sentences*	They had coffee **and** dessert. She likes coffee, **but** she doesn't like tea.
Noun (n)		**David** walked to **school**. The **dictionary** is on the **table**.
Preposition (prep)		I work **at** a bank. The store is **on** Madison Avenue **in** New York.
Pronoun (pron)		Pam is tired. **She** is going to bed early. Mr. and Mrs. Owen own a store. **They** sell furniture.
Verb (v)		Luke **ran** all the way home from school. He always **forgets** his books.

B. **Compare answers with the class. Are they the same?**

A. *What parts of speech are these words? Write "verb," "noun," "preposition," "adjective," or "adverb." Use your dictionary to help you. Some words can be more than one part of speech.*

1. guess _____ _____

2. kind _____ _____

3. organ _____

4. with _____

5. long _____ _____ _____

6. park _____ _____

7. damage _____ _____

8. seldom _____

9. patient _____ _____

10. iron _____ _____ _____

B. *Compare answers with another student. Are they the same?*

Read each sentence. What part of speech is the underlined word? Circle the correct answer. Use your dictionary to help you.

1. My brother got a ticket for driving <u>fast</u>.   adjective   (adverb)

2. Samantha is a <u>fast</u> learner.   adjective   adverb

3. Luis has <u>blue</u> eyes.   adjective   noun

4. <u>Blue</u> is his favorite color.   adjective   noun

5. The teacher lost <u>control</u> of the class.   noun   verb

6. My grandfather <u>controls</u> the family business.   noun   verb

7. The <u>show</u> starts in ten minutes.   noun   verb

8. He <u>showed</u> me how to fix my computer.   noun   verb

9. He <u>complimented</u> me on my essay.   noun   verb

10. I got several <u>compliments</u> on my new jacket.   noun   verb

Finding the Right Meaning

Many English words have more than one meaning. Your dictionary will give you all the meanings for each word.

Example:

> **fine**[1] /faɪn/ *adjective*
> **1** good enough or acceptable: *Your work is fine.* | *"I'll give the book back to you tomorrow." "That's fine."* SYNONYMS: **Okay, all right**
> **2** healthy and happy: *"How are you?" "Fine, thanks."*
> **3** very thin or made of very small pieces: *The desk was covered with a fine layer of dust.*
> **4** very good: *You're doing a fine job, and I'm really pleased with you.*
> **5** if the weather is fine, it is sunny and pleasant, with no rain: *It was a fine morning, so we decided to go for a walk along the beach.* SYNONYM: **fair**
>
> **fine**[2] *noun*
> money that you have to pay as a punishment for breaking a law or rule: *The company had to pay a fine for polluting the river.*
>
> **fine**[3] *verb*
> to make someone pay money as a punishment: *He was fined $50 for driving too fast.*

When the different meanings of a word are different parts of speech, the dictionary lists separate entries. Notice that *fine* has three separate entries. What part of speech is each entry?

First entry: _____   Second entry: _____

Third entry: _____

When the different meanings are the same part of speech, each meaning is numbered. There are five meanings for the adjective *fine*, but only one meaning for the noun and one meaning for the verb.

It is important to find the right definition, but it is sometimes difficult. Here are some hints to help you find the right definition.

- Look at the part of speech. The part of speech will help you find the correct meaning.

- Look at the order of the different meanings. The most common meaning is first.

- Read example sentences. They can help you understand the different meanings of a word.

EXERCISE 5

A. *Read all the definitions for the word "field." Write the part of speech and the meaning of "field" in each sentence. Follow the example in number 1.*

1. Dr. Lourie is an expert in the field of chemistry.

   Part of speech: _Noun_

   Meaning: _a subject that people study, or a type of work_

2. All we saw for miles and miles were fields of corn.

   Part of speech: _____

   Meaning: _____

   _____

3. There are many coal fields in the Appalachian Mountains.

   Part of speech: _____

   Meaning: _____

   _____

> **field** /fild/ *noun*
> **1** an area of land in the country where crops are grown or animals feed on grass: *There were fields of wheat for mile after mile.*
> **2** an area of ground where sports are played: *a baseball field | The team ran out on the field.*
> **3** a subject that people study, or a type of work: *Professor Kramer is an expert in the field of biology.*
> **4** **oil/gas/coal field** = an area where there is a lot of oil, gas, or coal under the ground

4. The whole team ran onto the field after they won the soccer game.

   Part of speech: _____

   Meaning: _____

B. *Compare answers with another student. Are they the same?*

A. *Find the underlined words in the dictionary entry. Read all the definitions for the word. Write the part of speech and the meaning of the word for each sentence.*

1. The owners built a new kitchen in the apartment. Then they <u>raised</u> the rent.

   Part of speech: _____

   Meaning: _____

   _____

2. Larry <u>raised</u> his glass and made a toast to the newlyweds.

   Part of speech: _____

   Meaning: _____

   _____

3. After three years, I finally got a <u>raise</u> at work.

   Part of speech: _____

   Meaning: _____

4. The employees <u>raised</u> questions at the meeting.

   Part of speech: _____

   Meaning: _____

5. We sold candy and <u>raised</u> $500 for the library.

   Part of speech: _____

   Meaning: _____

6. Mrs. Rand <u>raised</u> her niece after her sister died.

   Part of speech: _____

   Meaning: _____

> **raise¹** /reɪz/ *verb*
> **1** to move something to a higher position: *He raised his arms above his head.* | *Raise your hand if you know the answer.*
> **2** to increase something: *They raised the price from $1.99 to $3.99.*
> **3** to take care of children, animals, or crops until they are grown: *She raised three sons on her own.*
> **4** to collect money to help people: *The kids raised $400 for the school by washing cars.*
> **5** to begin to talk or write about something that you want people to think about: *The students raised several questions during the discussion.*
>
> **raise²** *noun*
> an increase in the money you earn: *She asked her boss for a raise after a year.*

B. *Compare answers with another student. Are they the same?*

A. *Find the underlined words in the dictionary entry. Read all the definitions for the word. Write the part of speech and the meaning of the word for each sentence.*

board¹ /bɔrd/ *noun*
1 a flat piece of wood or plastic that you use for writing or doing things on: *The new teacher wrote her name on the board. | Chop the carrots on a cutting board. | a chess board*
2 a long flat piece of wood used for making floors, walls, fences, etc.: *He cut two 6-foot boards in half with a saw.*
3 the group of people who make the rules and important decisions for a school or organization: *The school board is discussing pay with the teachers' union.*
4 on board = on an airplane, ship, train, or bus: *There were over 500 passengers on board when the boat sank.*
5 the meals that are provided for you when you pay to stay somewhere: *College students have to pay for room and board to stay in the dormitories.*

board² *verb*
to get on an airplane, ship, train, or bus in order to travel somewhere: *The passengers were waiting to board the plane.* SYNONYM: **get on**

1. We're building a bookcase. We need two more wooden <u>boards</u>.

   Part of speech: _____

   Meaning: _____

2. My father is the chairman of the <u>board</u> of directors.

   Part of speech: _____

   Meaning: _____

3. Paula's scholarship will pay her tuition, and her room and <u>board</u>.

Part of speech: _____

Meaning: _____

4. We will <u>board</u> the plane in fifteen minutes.

Part of speech: _____

Meaning: _____

5. The professor wrote the formula on the <u>board</u>.

Part of speech: _____

Meaning: _____

6. Luckily, there were no passengers on <u>board</u> the ship when it sank.

Part of speech: _____

Meaning: _____

B. *Compare answers with another student. Are they the same?*

Spelling and Irregular Forms of Words

Spelling words correctly is important for writers. You probably already know some rules for spelling words in English. But English also has irregular spelling of many words. How do you know the right way to spell these words? Your dictionary can help you check the spelling.

> **Remember**
>
> Write down new words in your vocabulary notebook or on flash cards. Include the correct spelling of the different forms of the word. *(See Part 4, Unit 1, for more information on using vocabulary notebooks and flash cards.)*

Work in a group. Read the dictionary entry. Discuss the questions. Write the answers.

---

cry¹ /kraɪ/ *verb* (**cried, cries**)
1 if you cry, tears come out of your eyes because you are hurt or unhappy: *Sad movies always make me cry.*
2 if a baby cries, it makes a loud sound: *The baby started crying again.*
3 (also **cry out**) to shout something loudly: *"Wait for me!" she cried. | The boy cried out for help.*

cry² *noun* (plural **cries**)
1 a loud sound you make when you are hurt, frightened, or very happy: *She gave a sudden cry of pain.*
2 a loud shout: *There was a cry of "Stop, thief!"*
3 a sound that some animals or birds make: *Outside, I could hear the cry of seagulls.*

---

1. What parts of speech is the word *cry?* _____
_____

2. How many different meanings does the noun have?_____

3. How many different meanings does the verb have? _____

4. Is *cry* spelled correctly in the sentence below? _____

   I saw a sad movie last night. I cryed and cryed.

   How do you know? _____

5. Is *cry* spelled correctly in the sentence below? _____

   She always cries at sad movies.

   How do you know? _____

6. What is the plural of the noun *cry?* _____

   How do you know? _____

A. *Use your dictionary. Write the correct spelling of these words. Follow the examples in numbers 1 and 2.*

1. (thin+-er)   _thinner_
2. (worry +-ed)   _worried_
3. (funny +-est)   _____
4. (surprise +-ing)   _____
5. (plan +-ed)   _____
6. (enthusiastic +-ly) _____
7. (knife +-s)   _____

B. *Complete the sentences. Use the words in Exercise A.*

1. Nick looks great now. He looked _thinner_ last year.
2. You were very late. I was _worried_ .
3. He is the _____ student in the class.
4. I got some _____ news today.
5. She _____ a surprise birthday party for her husband.
6. Carol spoke _____ about her new idea.
7. All of these _____ are dirty. Please wash them.

C. *Compare answers with another student. Are they the same?*

Spelling and Irregular Forms of Nouns

Most plural nouns in English are formed by adding an *-s*, *-es*, or *-ies* to the end of the noun. But some nouns are irregular. The dictionary gives the spelling of irregular plural nouns.

Work with a partner. Read the dictionary entry. Discuss the questions. Write the answers.

---

lead·er /ˈlidɚ/ *noun*
1 the person who is in charge of a country or group of people: *The meeting will be attended by many world leaders, including the president.*
2 the person or team that is winning a race or competition: *She was the leader for the first half of the race.*

lead·ing /ˈlidɪŋ/ *adjective*
most important or most successful: *He got a leading part in the play.*

leaf /lif/ *noun* (plural **leaves** /livz/)
one of the flat, green parts of a plant or tree, that grows from its stem or branches: *There are still some leaves on the trees, but most of them have fallen off.*

leaf·let /ˈliflɪt/ *noun*
a piece of paper with information or an advertisement printed on it: *They gave out leaflets in the street for the restaurant.*

league /lig/ *noun*
1 a group of sports teams that play against each other in order to see who is best: *How many teams are in the National Football League?*
2 a group of people or countries that have joined together to achieve something: *the League of Women Voters*

---

1. Which noun has an irregular plural? _____

2. Which two sentences are correct? Check (✓) them. How do you know?

☐ There are several national baseball leagues in the United States.

☐ I raked the leafs and put them in a big pile.

☐ I have three leavelets from the new Italian restaurant.

☐ Some of the leaves fell off the tree.

A. *Use your dictionary. Write the plural form of each noun.*

1. tooth   *teeth*   6. foot   _____

2. goose   _____   7. deer   _____

3. person   _____   8. cactus   _____

4. ox   _____   9. mouse   _____

5. child   _____   10. woman   _____

B. *Choose three of the words from Exercise A. Write a sentence for each word. Use the plural form of each word.*

Example:

The dentist checked my teeth.

1. _____

2. _____

3. _____

C. *Share your sentences with a partner. Are they correct?*

Spelling and Irregular Forms of Verbs

Most verbs in English form the simple past by adding *-ed* , *-d,* or *-ied* to the base form of the verb. But some verbs are irregular. Your dictionary will give you the past form for irregular verbs.

A. *Use a dictionary. Write the simple past of each verb.*

1. pay   *paid*   6. catch   _____

2. wear   _____   7. cut   _____

3. bring   _____   8. feel   _____

4. choose   _____   9. fight   _____

5. write   _____   10. understand   _____

B. Choose three of the words from Exercise A. Write a sentence for each word. Use the simple past of each word.

Example:

I paid all of my bills online.

1. _____
2. _____
3. _____

C. Share sentences with a partner. Are they correct?

Formal and Informal Words

Most English words can be either formal or informal. Some words and phrases are informal. We don't usually use them in academic writing. Other words are more formal. The dictionary tells you when a word or phrase is formal or informal.

EXERCISE 13

A. The two words in parentheses have similar meanings. Circle the more formal word. Use your dictionary to help you. Follow the example in number 1.

1. (Kids / Children) in the United States usually go to school until they are eighteen years old.

2. The (police officers / cops) arrived a few minutes after the accident.

3. I invited several of my (friends / buddies) to the conference.

4. She got (expelled from / kicked out of) school. She cheated on an exam.

5. The ticket to the concert costs thirty-five (bucks / dollars).

6. I keep my art (supplies / stuff) in the closet.

7. Mark decided to (quit / resign) and look for another job.

8. Paula (arrived / showed up) an hour late.

B. Compare answers with another student. Are they the same?

Synonyms and Antonyms

Learning synonyms and antonyms with new words will help you increase your vocabulary. It will also make your writing more interesting. You can find synonyms and antonyms for some words in your dictionary. The synonym or antonym is usually listed at the end of the entry.

A **synonym** is a word with the same or similar meaning as another word. For example, *near* and *close* are synonyms.

An **antonym** is a word that means the opposite of another word. For example, *near* and *far* are opposites.

Example:

> **cour•age** /ˈkɚ•ɪdʒ/ *noun*
> the quality of being brave: *I didn't have the courage to ask my boss for a raise.* SYNONYM: **bravery**
> —**courageous** /kəˈreɪdʒəs/ *adjective* brave: *his courageous battle against the disease*
> —**courageously** *adverb* in a brave way: *The soldiers defended the town courageously.*
> [ORIGIN: 1200–1300 From the Latin word *cor*, which means "heart."]

This dictionary entry gives a lot of information about the word *courage*. What synonym is listed for *courage*? _____

EXERCISE 14

Use your dictionary. Find synonyms for these words. There may be more than one synonym.

1. courage ___bravery___   6. foolish _____

2. additional _____   7. gem _____

3. beneath _____   8. prison _____

4. certain _____   9. remark _____

5. chance _____   10. sofa _____

A. *Work with a partner. Rewrite the sentences. Replace the underlined word with a synonym. Use a dictionary to help you choose the best synonym.*

1. I was <u>sad</u> when my boyfriend broke up with me.

   I was upset when my boyfriend broke up with me.

2. The school has a lot of <u>new</u> technology.

   _____

3. I don't want to use that <u>dirty</u> bathroom.

   _____

4. The snake <u>frightened</u> the little boy.

   _____

5. Wow! You look <u>nice</u> in that dress.

   _____

6. Did you <u>see</u> a police car?

   _____

7. They live in a <u>small</u> two-room apartment.

   _____

8. You need to be <u>thin</u> to look good in that dress.

   _____

9. A <u>smart</u>, young scientist discovered the new medicine.

   _____

10. Sarah's parents were <u>happy</u> at her graduation.

    _____

B. *Join another pair. Compare sentences. Did you choose the same synonyms?*

Match each word in Column A with its antonym in Column B.

A	B
1. hazy	___ **a.** professional
2. long	___ **b.** rude
3. amateur	___ **c.** ineffective
4. gain	_1_ **d.** clear
5. effective	___ **e.** short
6. polite	___ **f.** lose

Answer the questions. Begin each answer with "No" and use an antonym of the underlined word. Follow the example in number 1.

1. Do you think the math test was <u>easy</u>?

   No. I thought it was difficult.

2. Is this coffee <u>strong</u>?

_____

3. Are the clothes in the dryer still <u>wet</u>?

_____

4. Do your parents live <u>close</u> to here?

_____

5. Is this the <u>shallow</u> end of the pool?

_____

6. Is your daughter <u>tall</u> for her age?

_____

7. Does this movie take place in the <u>future</u>?

_____

8. Do you like to sit in the <u>back</u> of the room?

_____

Online and Electronic Dictionaries

There are many different kinds of dictionaries. Each kind of dictionary has advantages and disadvantages. Online and electronic dictionaries are often a good option for students learning English. You can find many online dictionaries on the Internet. Print dictionaries often have online versions that are free and easy to use. Many online dictionaries include audio pronunciation and pictures. Sometimes they also include video and links to interesting articles and blogs. Some students like to use electronic dictionaries. Some electronic dictionaries are apps on smartphones or electronic tablets. Others are special handheld devices (PEDs). Still others are CD-ROMs or DVD-ROMs that you can use on a computer.

EXERCISE 18

A. **Work with a group. Discuss these questions:**

1. Do you have an electronic dictionary or use an online dictionary?
2. If you answered "no":
   - What kind of dictionary do you usually use?
   - Would you like to use an electronic or online dictionary?
3. If you answered "yes":
   - What kind of dictionary do you use (online or electronic, or both)?
   - How often do you use it?
   - Do you like it?

B. **Work with your class. Discuss the advantages and disadvantages of electronic dictionaries. Complete the chart.**

Advantages	Disadvantages
You can hear how the word is pronounced.	Some are expensive.

C. *Discuss the advantages and disadvantages of online dictionaries. Complete the chart.*

Advantages	Disadvantages
You can hear how the word is pronounced.	

EXERCISE 19

A. **Go to the website http://www.ldoceonline.com/. Type the word "stamp" in the search box. Make a list of information you find.**

_____

_____

_____

_____

B. *Work with a partner. Compare answers. Are they the same? Is the information helpful?*

C. *Now, type the word "doubt" in the search box. Make a list of information you find.*

_____

_____

_____

_____

D. **Compare your answers to Exercise C with another student. Are they the same? Is the information helpful?**

Word Parts

Many English words have several parts. The main part of an English word is the root. Some words add parts to the root. These parts are prefixes and suffixes. They change or add to the meaning of the root.

A **root** is the basic part of the word. It gives the basic meaning.

- *kind*

A **prefix** is a group of letters that is added to the beginning of a word.

- ***un*** + *kind* = *unkind*

A **suffix** is a group of letters added to the end of a word.

- *kind* + ***ness*** = *kindness*

In this unit, you will learn some common prefixes and suffixes.

Warm Up

Uni–, *bi–*, and *tri–* are all prefixes. When they are added to the word *cycle*, they change the meaning.

A. ***Look at the pictures. Complete each sentence on the next page with a word from the box.***

| unicycle | bicycle | tricycle |

1. The woman is riding a _____.
2. The child is riding a _____.
3. The man is riding a _____.

B. **Work with a partner. Discuss these questions:**

- What do all the words in the box have in common?
- How is each word different?
- What do you think *uni-* means?
- What do you think *bi-* means?
- What do you think *tri-* means?

PREFIXES

There are several common prefixes in English. Two of the most common are *un-* and *re-*. You can add these prefixes to the beginning of adjectives and verbs. When you add them to a word, the meaning of the word changes.

The Prefix *Un-*

Un- is the most common prefix in English. *Un-* has several meanings.

- The prefix *un-* usually means "not." You can add it to an adjective.
  Example:
  kind (adjective)
  unkind (adjective. It is the antonym of *kind*. It means "not kind.")

- The prefix *un-* can also mean "do the opposite of" an action. You can add it to a verb to talk about the opposite action.
  Example:
  tie (verb)
  untie (verb. It is the antonym of *tie*. It means "do the opposite of" *tie*.)

(See Part 4, Unit 2, to learn more about antonyms.)

A. *Add the prefix "un-" to each word. Follow the example in number 1.*

1. clear   _unclear_   7. comfortable _____

2. sure   _____   8. kind   _____

3. happy   _____   9. able   _____

4. lock   _____   10. lucky   _____

5. fair   _____   11. pack   _____

6. tie   _____   12. usual   _____

B. *Write the correct word for each definition. Use the words from Exercise A.*

1. not clear   _unclear_

2. not kind   _____

3. the opposite of lock   _____

4. the opposite of tie   _____

5. not able   _____

6. not sure   _____

7. the opposite of pack   _____

8. not fair   _____

9. not comfortable   _____

10. not lucky   _____

11. not happy   _____

12. not usual   _____

C. Complete the sentences. Use your answers from Exercise A.

1. You need to _____ the shoelaces before you take off your shoes.

2. He didn't raise his hand because he was _____ of the answer.

3. I don't understand this message. The meaning is _____.

4. I never win at card games. I'm just _____.

5. I can't sleep in this bed. It's very _____.

6. I'm sorry, but I'm _____ to go to the meeting.

7. It's _____ for men to get paid more than women for the same job.

8. Pam is almost always on time. It's _____ for her to be late for class.

9. The little girl is crying. She is _____ about something.

10. My black pants are still in the suitcase. I didn't _____.

11. Cindy had an argument with her boyfriend. She said some very _____ things to him.

12. I forgot my keys. Now I can't _____ the door.

D. Work in a group. Discuss the questions. Write your answers in complete sentences.

1. Do you think any numbers are unlucky? Which ones?

_____

2. What kind of shoes do you think are uncomfortable?

_____

3. What is an unusual animal in your country?

_____

A. *Work in a group. Discuss the meaning of the verbs. Then match the verbs to the correct noun phrases. Follow the example in number 1.*

Verbs	Noun Phrases
1. untie	_____ **a.** the car door
2. unlock	_____ **b.** a shirt
3. unwrap	_____ **c.** the coffee pot
4. unpack	_____ **d.** the birthday present
5. unbutton	_1_ **e.** his shoe laces
6. unplug	_____ **f.** your seat belt
7. unfasten	_____ **g.** my suitcase

Remember

Look up the meaning of new words in a dictionary. Words are listed in alphabetical order. Look for words with the prefix *un-* under the letter *u*, or the first letter of the root word.

B. *Write complete sentences. Use the verbs and noun phrases in Exercise A. Follow the example in number 1.*

1. *The little boy can't untie his shoelaces.* _____
2. _____
3. _____
4. _____
5. _____
6. _____
7. _____

C. *Share sentences with another student.*

The Prefix *Re-*

The prefix *re-* is the second most common prefix in English. The prefix *re-* means "again." Add *re-* to verbs. It means "do the action of the verb again."

Examples:

re + read = reread (to read again)

re + tell = retell (to tell again)

re + write = rewrite (to write again)

EXERCISE 3

A. Add the prefix "re-" to each word.

1. fuel _____   4. build _____

2. charge _____   5. write _____

3. heat _____

B. Complete each sentence with the correct word from Exercise A.

1. I made a lot of mistakes in this essay. I need to _____ it.

2. This coffee is cold. Please _____ it for me.

3. I have to _____ the battery on my phone.

4. We stop in Los Angeles to _____ the plane. Then we fly to Hawaii.

5. The storm destroyed our garage. We need to _____ it.

EXERCISE 4

A. Match the verbs to the correct noun phrases. Follow the example in number 1.

Verbs		Noun Phrases
1. retake	____	**a.** a letter
2. retie	____	**b.** his store
3. retype	_1_	**c.** the test
4. recycle	____	**d.** my shoelaces
5. reboot	____	**e.** these plastic bottles
6. reopen	____	**f.** my computer

B. Write complete sentences. Use the verbs and noun phrases in Exercise A. Follow the example in number 1.

1. _*They need to retake the test.*_

2. _____

3. _____

4. _____

5. _____

6. _____

C. Compare sentences with another student. Are they the same?

SUFFIXES

A **suffix** is a letter or group of letters you add to the end of a word. You already know some English suffixes and use them in your writing. Suffixes can:

- Change a word from one part of speech to another part of speech.
  Examples:
  Adding the suffix "-ly" can change an adjective to an adverb
  nice (adjective) → *nice**ly*** (adverb)

- Change the verb from the present tense to the past tense.
  Examples:
  Adding the suffix "-ed" changes these regular verbs from present to past
  *hope – hop**ed***
  *learn – learn**ed***

- Change a word from singular to plural.
  Examples:
  Adding the suffix "-s" or "-es" changes these singular nouns to plural nouns
  *box – box**es***
  *movie – movi**es***

- Change the meaning of a word.
  Examples:
  Adding the suffix "-er" changes the meaning of the word "teach"
  *teach – teach**er***
  Adding the suffix "-ful" changes the meaning of the word "care"
  *care – care**ful***

The Suffixes -*Ful* and -*Less*

Two common suffixes in English are **-*ful*** and **-*less***. The suffix -*less* means "without" and the suffix -*ful* means "full of." Add these suffixes to nouns to make adjectives.

Examples:

Noun   Adjective
hope + *ful* = *hopeful* (full of hope)

Noun   Adjective
hope + *less* = *hopeless* (without hope)

EXERCISE 5

Work with a partner. Complete the chart. Follow the example.

Root	-ful	-less
thought	*thoughtful*	*thoughtless*
harm		
pain		
help		
use		
care		
power		

Remember

Look up the meaning of new words in a dictionary. Words are listed in alphabetical order. Look for words with suffixes under the first letter of the root word. (*See Part 4, Unit 2, for more information on alphabetical order.*)

A. *Complete each sentence with the correct word in parentheses.*

1. I have a bad toothache. It is really __*painful*__ .
   (painful / painless)

2. Smoking has many _____ effects on your body.
   (harmful / harmless)

3. I don't like this website. It has a lot of _____ information.
   (useful / useless)

4. Please be _____ when you drive home. The roads are wet.
   (careful / careless)

5. The president of a country has a _____ job.
   (powerful / powerless)

6. Thank you for the gift. It was so _____ .
   (thoughtful / thoughtless)

7. Babies are _____ in many ways. They need protection.
   (helpful / helpless)

B. *Compare answers with another student. Are they the same?*

A. *Work with a partner. Write a sentence with each word.*

1. careless

_____

2. thoughtless

_____

3. painless

_____

4. helpful

_____

5. useful

_____

6. harmless

_____

7. powerless

_____

B. *Share your sentences with the class.*

The Suffixes -Er, -Or, -Ist

English has several suffixes that mean "someone who." The most common ones are
-er, -or, and *-ist*. Add *-er* or *-or* to the end of a verb. The new word describes the
person who does the action of the verb.

Examples:

> *write – writer*
>
> *act – actor*

Add *-ist* to the name of an instrument or a profession. The new word is the name of
a person who plays an instrument or who has certain professions.

Examples:

> *guitar – guitarist*
>
> *manicure – manicurist*

> **Remember**
>
> Sometimes the spelling of a word changes when we add a suffix. Use
> your dictionary to check the correct spelling and use of suffixes.

EXERCISE 8

Underline the suffixes.

1. Peter inspects buildings. He is a building inspector.

2. Mark teaches science at the university. He is a scientist.

3. Jocelyn designs clothes. She is a well-known fashion designer.

4. Mohammed reports information for a newspaper. He is a
   newspaper reporter.

5. Paula is an artist. She shows her art in a gallery downtown.

Work with a partner. Complete the chart. Write the word that describes the person. Use the hints and a dictionary to help you. Follow the example.

Hint	The Person
swim	*swimmer*
violin	
piano	
translate	
edit	
teach	
bake	
drive	

Remember

Learn the spelling of words with suffixes. Write the words in your vocabulary notebook. *(See Part 4, Unit 1, for more information on using vocabulary notebooks.)*

WORD FAMILIES

A **word family** is a group of words that look similar. They have the same root. Words in a word family have related meanings, but the words are different parts of speech. Learning words from the same family will help you expand your vocabulary. Look at the word family for the word *interest*.

Noun	Verb	Adjective	Adverb
interest	interest	interesting / interested	X

Sometimes the same word is more than one part of speech.

Example:

interest (noun)

interest (verb)

Some word families have more than one form for a part of speech.
Example:
  interested (adjective)
  interesting (adjective)

Some word families do not have words for every part of speech.
Example:
  There is no adverb form in the *interest* word family.

Here are some common word families.

Noun	Verb	Adjective	Adverb
difference	differ	different	differently
care	care	careful	carefully
cooperation	cooperate	cooperative	cooperatively
help	help	helpful	helpfully
information	inform	informative	X

(See Part 4, Unit 2, for more on parts of speech.)

EXERCISE 10

A. Complete each sentence. Circle and write the correct word.

1. The sidewalk is icy. Please walk _____ .

   a. care   **b.** careful   **c.** carefully

2. "What do you want to eat?" "I don't _____ ."

   a. care   **b.** careful   **c.** carefully

3. My mother is a _____ driver.

   a. care   **b.** careful   **c.** carefully

4. This website has a lot of _____ information.

   a. help   **b.** helpful   **c.** helpfully

5. I can _____ you move this table.

   a. help   **b.** helpful   **c.** helpfully

(continued)

6. Ask your teacher for _____.

    a. help   **b.** helpful   **c.** helpfully

7. Everyone worked _____ to solve the problem.

    a. cooperate   **b.** cooperation   **c.** cooperatively

8. Let's _____ and work together.

    a. cooperate   **b.** cooperation   **c.** cooperatively

9. _____ is important for successful teamwork.

    a. Cooperate   **b.** Cooperation   **c.** Cooperatively

10. She plays several _____ sports.

    a. differ   **b.** different   **c.** differently

11. British English and American English _____ in a few ways.

    a. differ   **b.** different   **c.** differently

12. There is a big _____ between the two brothers.

    a. differ   **b.** different   **c.** difference

13. Please complete the form with the correct _____.

    a. inform   **b.** informative   **c.** information

14. This article is very _____. I learned a lot from it.

    a. inform   **b.** informative   **c.** information

15. The pilot will _____ us when the plane is landing.

    a. inform   **b.** informative   **c.** information

B. *Compare answers with another student. Are they the same?*

EXERCISE 11

A. *Work with a partner. Complete the chart on the next page. Use nouns and verbs from the box. Make a guess if you aren't sure. Follow the example.*

~~communicate~~	decide	memorize	student	succeed
communication	decision	memory	study	success

Noun	Verb
	communicate

B. *Use your dictionary. Find the adjective form for these words. Then write a sentence using the adjective.*

1. study _____

_____

2. success _____

_____

3. memory _____

_____

Further Practice

Journal, Blog, and Vocabulary Notebook Idea

- Write a journal or blog about one of these questions. Try to use five new words from this unit.
  - What is a special memory from your childhood?
  - What is the most memorable day of your childhood?
  - Who is the most studious person you know?
  - Where do you like to study? Why?
  - What are some tips for being a successful student?
- Write the new words in your vocabulary notebook. Then use them to make flash cards.

How Words Work Together

It is important to learn the meaning of new words. But it is not always enough to learn words separately. You also need to learn how words work together. Different languages put words together in different ways. English has many phrases and groups of words that go together. In this unit, you will learn some of the most common ones. You will also learn ways to remember them.

Learning words that go together in English will improve your fluency and make your writing sound more natural.

Warm Up

A.   *Match the pictures with the phrases. Write the number of the picture.*

1   2

_____ Doing Homework

_____ Making Friends

B.   *Work in a group. Discuss these questions:*

- How do you say *make friends* in your language?
- How do you say *do your homework*?
- In your language, do you use the same verb for these phrases?

PHRASES WITH VERBS

In English, some very common verbs pair with certain nouns. *Make, do, have, take, play,* and *go* are some of these verbs. It is important to know which nouns go with these verbs, and which nouns do not.

The best way to learn these phrases is to practice them. You can write them in your vocabulary notebook and make flash cards. You can use them in your journal or blog. You can also make a list or chart of words that go together. Practice them often and they will not be difficult to remember.

Make and *Do*

Make and *do* are common verbs in English, but they can be confusing. We use the verb *make* in certain phrases and *do* in other phrases.

> **Examples:**
>
> I ***made a new friend*** at the library.
>
> I ***did my homework*** at the library.

In English we say ***make*** friends, but ***do*** homework.

EXERCISE 1

Read the conversation between a husband and wife. Underline the phrases with "make" and "do." Follow the example.

Susan: I'll <u>make dinner</u>. Will you <u>do the dishes</u>?

Jack: I don't like doing dishes. I'll do the laundry instead.

Susan: No way! Last time you made a big mistake. You washed my favorite sweater with hot water, and it shrank!

(continued)

Jack:	Well, I'm not good at doing chores.
Susan:	Come on, Jack. Stop making excuses.
Jack:	At least I make the bed every day.
Susan:	OK, let's make a deal. I'll do the grocery shopping, and I'll do the dishes. You make dinner.
Jack:	Can I make a suggestion? Let's go out to dinner instead.
Susan:	Good idea! Where should we go?
Jack:	You make the decision. I always decide.
Susan:	Let's try the new Chinese restaurant.
Jack:	OK. Do me a favor? Call and make a reservation for seven o'clock.
Susan:	Deal! It's nice doing business with you!

EXERCISE 2

Work in a group. Complete the chart with words from the box. Use the sentences in Exercise 1 to help you. Follow the examples.

a~~ deal~~	a reservation	chores	the laundry
a decision	a suggestion	dinner	the shopping
a~~ favor~~	an excuse	the bed	
a mistake	business	the dishes	

Make	Do
a deal	*a favor*

A. *Complete the sentences. Write the correct word.*

1. I hate _____ my homework late at night.
   (doing / making)

2. Let's _____ dinner at my house.
   (make / do)

3. Did you _____ your plane reservation?
   (do / make)

4. I want to _____ my decision today.
   (do / make)

5. Stop _____ excuses for being late.
   (making / doing)

6. I don't have any clean clothes. It's time to _____ the laundry.
   (make / do)

7. The receptionist _____ a mistake. Your appointment is at noon.
   (made / did)

8. Please _____ me a favor and give this book to Tom.
   (make / do)

B. *Compare answers with another student. Are they the same?*

C. *Choose three phrases with "make" and three phrases with "do" from Exercises 2 and 3A. Make flash cards for these six phrases.*

(See Part 4, Unit 1, for more information on flash cards.)

EXERCISE 4

A. *Work with another student. Write a short conversation on a separate piece of paper. Use four phrases with "make" or "do."*

B. *Share your conversation with another pair. Take turns. Role-play the conversations.*

Have and Take

Have and *take* are also common verbs in English. They are also sometimes confusing. We use the verb *have* in certain phrases and *take* in other phrases.

Examples:

*I **have** a bad toothache.*

***Take** two aspirins and call the dentist.*

In English we say ***have** a toothache*, but ***take** an aspirin*.

*Read the conversation between friends. Underline the phrases with "take"
and "have." Follow the example.*

Ruth: I'm so glad you suggested that we <u>have lunch</u> together. I'm sorry
I'm late.

Pam: Did you have trouble finding the restaurant?

Ruth: No, it was easy. I took the bus. But a taxi had an accident, so
some streets were closed.

Pam: So, do you have any ideas about Jason's thirtieth birthday? What
do you want to do?

Ruth: Let's have a surprise party for him.

Pam: He's going to take a vacation with his family soon.

Ruth: Then let's plan the party for next weekend.

Pam: Good idea.

Ruth: I'll make phone calls and invite everyone.

Pam: Great. I just bought a new camera, so I'll take pictures at
the party.

Ruth: I love surprises!

Read the conversation between friends. Underline the phrases with "take" and "have."

Mark: It's 5:30. I'm tired and hungry.

Steve: OK. Let's take a break. But first, let's finish taking notes. There are so many names and dates to learn.

Mark: We need to know so much before we take the test on Monday.

Steve: I know. We also need to study the maps.

Mark: Listen. Maybe we can do all that after we have dinner. I just want to eat or take a nap right now.

Steve: There is so much to do.

Mark: I have a headache, too!

Steve: Why don't you take an aspirin?

Mark: Wait. I have a plan. Let's take some time off. We can go out and have fun tonight. Then we can study all weekend.

Steve: Really? You want to study all weekend?

Work in a group. Complete the chart with words from the box. Use the sentences in Exercises 5 and 6 to help you. Follow the examples.

~~a break~~	a plan	an aspirin	lunch	time off
~~a headache~~	a test	an idea	notes	trouble
a nap	a vacation	dinner	pictures	
a party	an accident	fun	the bus	

Have	Take
a headache	a break

How Words Work Together **233**

A. **Work with another student. Write a short conversation on a separate piece of paper. Use three phrases with "take" and three phrases with "have."**

B. **Share your conversation with another pair. Take turns. Role-play the conversations.**

EXERCISE 9

Complete the sentences. Use the verbs from the box. Some verbs are used more than once.

make	do	have	take

1. The next time we _____ a vacation, let's go to Paris.

2. First, I have to _____ my homework. Then, I'll relax and watch TV.

3. Kim always _____ fun with her friends.

4. The roads are wet. Drive carefully. Don't _____ an accident.

5. Did you _____ a decision about graduate school yet?

6. Will you _____ me a favor and drive me to school today?

7. I drank too much coffee, and now I _____ a headache.

Play and *Go*

We use the verbs *play* and *go* with phrases about sports and other activities. Use *play* with ball sports or competitive games. In competitive games, you play against another person. Use *go* with activities that end in *-ing* and that you usually do alone.

Examples:
> I **play soccer** with my friends.
> I **go skiing** in Vermont every winter.

A. *Complete the sentences. Circle the correct letter and write the word on the line. Follow the example in number 1.*

1. I __go_____ jogging when the weather is nice.

   a. play

   (b.) go

2. Jeff and I _____ tennis every week.

   a. play

   b. go

3. Are you _____ surfing on Sunday?

   a. playing

   b. going

4. She _____ sailing in the summer.

   a. plays

   b. goes

5. He enjoys _____ chess with his grandfather.

   a. playing

   b. going

6. He _____ ice hockey in college.

   a. played

   b. went

7. We are _____ fishing next Saturday.

   a. playing

   b. going

B. *Compare answers with another student. Are they the same?*

PHRASES WITH NOUNS

Like verbs, many nouns appear in common phrases. When you hear or read a new phrase, look it up in a dictionary. Most dictionaries list these phrases under the noun or verb in the phrase. Study the phrases the way you study and review individual words.

Phrases with *Friend*

Friend is often paired with certain adjectives. These phrases with "adjective + *friend*" describe a type of friend, or a quality about the friend.

EXERCISE 11

Read the sentences. Underline the phrases with "friend" or "friends." Follow the example in number 1.

1. I have a wonderful circle of <u>true friends</u>.
2. Gail is my best friend. We are like sisters.
3. I met my fiancé through a mutual friend.
4. I got in touch with an old friend on Facebook.
5. Cathy is a fair-weather friend. She is never around when I'm having problems.
6. I only invited my close friends to the dinner party.

EXERCISE 12

A. Match the phrases to the definitions. Use the sentences in Exercise 11 to help you.

Phrases	Definitions
1. true friend	___ a. a friend for a long time
2. fair-weather friend	___ b. a friend to you and someone else you know
3. old friend	_1_ c. a friend all the time; a very good friend
4. close friend	___ d. a friend you can talk to and share personal things
5. mutual friend	___ e. the friend you like the most
6. best friend	___ f. a friend only some of the time; not a good friend

B. *Read the types of friends in the chart. Write the name of one of your friends for each type. Write sentences about your friends. Follow the example.*

Phrase	Sentence
old friend: Marie	Marie and I are old friends. We met twenty years ago. We were in school together, and we are still friends now.
best friend:	
true friend:	
mutual friend:	
fair-weather friend:	
close friend:	

C. *Work in a group. Share your sentences. Add sentences to the chart to help you remember the phrases.*

Phrases with *Time*

English has many words that are commonly used with the word *time*. Learning the words that go with *time* will help you build your vocabulary.

EXERCISE 13

Read the phrases in the box. Then underline the phrases with "time" in the sentences.

> ahead of time   have a good time   run out of time
> free time   on time   waste time

1. The show starts at three o'clock, but you should arrive ahead of time to get a good seat.

2. Don't waste time playing computer games all day. Do your homework instead.

3. I didn't do the last ten questions on the test. I ran out of time.

4. This bus is always on time, so I'm never late for work.

5. I hope you have a good time at the party. It'll be a lot of fun.

6. I like to play tennis in my free time.

EXERCISE 14

Match the phrases to the definitions. Use the sentences in Exercise 13 to help you.

Phrases	**Definitions**
1. run out of time	____ a. time when you aren't working
2. on time	____ b. use your time in a way that is not useful
3. ahead of time	____ c. enjoy yourself
4. free time	____ d. before the arranged or planned time
5. waste time	____ e. at the right time, not early or late
6. have a good time	_1_ f. not have enough time to finish something

A. *Complete the sentences. Circle the correct letter and write the word on the line. Follow the example in number 1.*

1. I ___go_____ jogging when the weather is nice.

   a. play

   (b.) go

2. Jeff and I _____ tennis every week.

   a. play

   b. go

3. Are you _____ surfing on Sunday?

   a. playing

   b. going

4. She _____ sailing in the summer.

   a. plays

   b. goes

5. He enjoys _____ chess with his grandfather.

   a. playing

   b. going

6. He _____ ice hockey in college.

   a. played

   b. went

7. We are _____ fishing next Saturday.

   a. playing

   b. going

B. *Compare answers with another student. Are they the same?*

PHRASES WITH NOUNS

Like verbs, many nouns appear in common phrases. When you hear or read a new phrase, look it up in a dictionary. Most dictionaries list these phrases under the noun or verb in the phrase. Study the phrases the way you study and review individual words.

Phrases with *Friend*

Friend is often paired with certain adjectives. These phrases with "adjective + *friend*" describe a type of friend, or a quality about the friend.

EXERCISE 11

Read the sentences. Underline the phrases with "friend" or "friends." Follow the example in number 1.

1. I have a wonderful circle of <u>true friends</u>.

2. Gail is my best friend. We are like sisters.

3. I met my fiancé through a mutual friend.

4. I got in touch with an old friend on Facebook.

5. Cathy is a fair-weather friend. She is never around when I'm having problems.

6. I only invited my close friends to the dinner party.

EXERCISE 12

A. Match the phrases to the definitions. Use the sentences in Exercise 11 to help you.

Phrases	Definitions
1. true friend	_____ **a.** a friend for a long time
2. fair-weather friend	_____ **b.** a friend to you and someone else you know
3. old friend	_1_ **c.** a friend all the time; a very good friend
4. close friend	_____ **d.** a friend you can talk to and share personal things
5. mutual friend	_____ **e.** the friend you like the most
6. best friend	_____ **f.** a friend only some of the time; not a good friend

A. *Complete the chart. Write your own sentences to help remember the phrases. Follow the example.*

Phrase	Sentence
on time	*Class starts at 10:00. I always arrive a few minutes late. I am never on time.*
ahead of time	
free time	
waste time	
run out of time	
have a good time	

B. *Work in a group. Share your sentences. Add sentences to the chart to help you remember the phrases.*

Remember

Use a vocabulary notebook and flash cards. They help you practice new vocabulary. Copy the charts with your sentences into your vocabulary notebook or write them on flash cards. Review them often.

(*See Part 4, Unit 1, for more information on strategies for building vocabulary.*)

Further Practice

Journal, Blog, and Vocabulary Notebook Ideas

- Write in your vocabulary notebooks.
  - Write phrases with the words *time* and *friend* from your reading in and out of class.
  - Listen for phrases with the words *time* and *friend* in conversations. Add the new phrases to your vocabulary notebook.
- Post lists on your class blog.
  - Make a list of ways to make new friends.
  - Make a list of ways to have fun in your city.
- Write a journal entry.
  - Write about making friends in a new place.
  - Write about wasting time. How do you waste time?

Creative Writing

Creative writing is a special kind of writing. In creative writing you write about personal feelings, ideas, and emotions. Poems, stories, and novels are examples of creative writing. Creative writing should be fun. It helps you increase your vocabulary and practice new ways of expressing yourself in English. Sometimes you can write a poem or a story with a partner or in a small group. This is a good way to share ideas in English.

In this unit, you will practice writing several kinds of poems. Try to use descriptive words in your writing. They add details and interest. Try to use the right words so your reader can understand your poems and stories.

Warm Up

Work with a partner. Discuss these questions:

- Do you like to write poems or stories in your language?

- Do you think it is easier (or more difficult) to write a poem than a paragraph in English? Why?

- Do you enjoy reading poems and stories? Would you rather read fiction or nonfiction?

- Who are the most famous poets from your country?

Robert Frost (1874–1963) was
a famous American poet.

WRITING CINQUAIN POEMS

A **cinquain** poem is a short poem with five lines. The word *cinquain* (pronounced "cin-kain") comes from the French word *cinq*, which means "five."

The topic of a cinquain poem is a noun. The noun is also the title of the poem. The rest of the poem describes that noun.

A cinquain poem has a special format.

This is the format of a cinquain poem:

Line 1: One noun. This word is the topic of the poem.
Line 2: Two adjectives that describe the noun.
Line 3: Three *-ing* verbs that go with the noun.
Line 4: A phrase or sentence with four words about the topic. This can be your feelings about the topic.
Line 5: A synonym for the topic or a word that relates to it.

Examples:

Clouds
Fluffy, white
Drifting, dancing, changing
Pictures in the sky
Dreams

Stars
Bright, silent
Shining, twinkling, shooting
Lighting up the night
Wishes

Hong Kong
Modern, ancient
Hoping, bustling, welcoming
Window to the world
Harbor

EXERCISE 1

A. *Look at the examples of cinquain poems on page 242. Read them silently as your teacher reads them aloud.*

B. *Use a dictionary. Look up words you do not know. Write them in your vocabulary notebook.*

C. *Work with a partner. Take turns reading the cinquain poems aloud.*

D. *Discuss these questions with your partner. Write the answers.*

1. What is the title of the first poem? _____

2. What is the title of the second poem? _____

3. What is the title of the third poem? _____

4. What part of speech are the words in the second line of each poem?

   _____

5. What three letters do all of the words in the third line of each

   poem end in? _____

6. The fourth line in each poem is a phrase. What does the phrase

   refer to? _____

7. How many words are in the fourth line? _____

8. Which is your favorite poem? Why? _____

   _____

A. **Work with a partner. Write a cinquain poem about the weather. Follow these steps.**

1. Think about this topic: Weather.

2. Describe the weather. Choose two words. Circle them.

beautiful	gusty	rainy	wet
black	happy	sad	white
chilly	hot	stormy	windy
cold	humid	sunny	

3. Think about your topic. What actions do you think about? What actions describe your topic? Choose three words. Circle them.

blowing	falling	shining
changing	lighting	shivering
drifting	melting	turning

4. Choose a phrase that describes your feelings about your topic. Circle it.

brings color to all	lighting up the sky
dark clouds rolling in	makes me feel alone
falling to the ground	makes the day happy
fun with my friends	puddles on the ground
in the dark night	the air smells nice

5. Choose a synonym or related word to your topic. Circle it.

blizzard	drizzle	humidity	slush	temperature
climate	fog	ice	sunshine	water

B. *Write your cinquain poem on the lines. Use your words in Exercise A.*

<u>Weather</u>
(noun)

_____ , _____
(adjective)   **(adjective)**

_____ , _____ , _____
(-*ing* verb)   **(-*ing* verb)**   **(-*ing* verb)**

_____
(a four-word phrase that expresses your feelings about the topic in line 1)

_____
(noun: synonym of the noun in line 1)

C. *Share your cinquain poem with your class.*

EXERCISE 3

A. *Write a cinquain poem. Follow these steps.*

1. Work with a partner. Read the list of topics for a poem. You can also brainstorm some other topics.

   - nature

   - a season (spring, summer, fall, winter)

   - weather

   - your favorite city

   - your hometown

   - a memory

   - a holiday

   - school

   - your job

   - _____

   - _____

   - _____

   - _____

2. Choose a topic for your poem: _____

(continued)

3. Think about your topic. What adjectives describe your topic? Write adjectives to answer these questions.

• What does your topic look like? _____

• What color is it? _____

• What does it smell like? Taste like? Sound like? Feel like?

_____

_____

4. What can your topic do? What actions describe your topic? (Use *-ing* verbs.)

_____

_____

_____

5. How do you feel about the topic? Write a phrase with four words that describes your feelings.

_____

6. What other word can you think of that relates to your topic? Is there a synonym for your topic?

_____

B. Write your cinquain poem on the lines. Use your words in Exercise A.

_____
(noun)

_____ , _____
(adjective)   (adjective)

_____ , _____ , _____
(-*ing* verb)   (-*ing* verb)   (-*ing* verb)

_____
(a four-word phrase that expresses your feelings about the topic in line 1)

_____
(noun: synonym of the noun in line 1)

C. Share your poem with your class.

WRITING TASK

> Write a cinquain poem.

    A. *Write a cinquain poem with another student or in a small group. Write your poem on a separate piece of paper.*

    B. *Choose one member of your pair or group to read the poem to the class.*

WRITING DIAMANTE POEMS

Diamante poems are also short poems. The word *diamante* comes from the French *diamant*, which means "diamond." Like cinquain poems, diamante poems have the shape of a diamond. Unlike cinquain poems, diamante poems have two topics. The first topic is the noun in line 1. The second topic is the noun in line 7. It is the opposite of the first topic.

A diamante poem is a poem about opposites. This is the format of a diamante poem:

Line 1: A noun. The topic of the poem and the opposite of line 7.
Line 2: Two adjectives that describe the noun in line 1.
Line 3: Three *-ing* verbs that describe the noun in line 1.
Line 4: Four nouns. Two nouns relate to line 1, the next two nouns relate to line 7.
Line 5: Three *-ing* verbs that describe the noun in line 7.
Line 6: Two adjectives that describe the noun in line 7.
Line 7: A noun. This is an antonym (opposite) of the noun in line 1.

Examples:

Sunrise ←
Golden, bright
Rising, shining, greeting
Morning, light, evening, shadow   Opposites
Falling, ending, relaxing
Calm, dark
Sunset ←

(continued)

Friend
Close, reliable
Caring, sharing, helping
Pal, partner, rival, foe
Fighting, hating, opposing
Fierce, angry
Enemy

Fire
Hot, smoky
Burning, roaring, blazing
Sparks, flame, crystal, frost
Freezing, shining, chilling
Cold, frozen
Ice

Remember

An **antonym** is a word with the opposite meaning of another word.
(See Part 4, Unit 2, for more information about antonyms.)

A. *Look at the examples of diamante poems on pages 247–248. Read them silently as your teacher reads them aloud.*

B. *Use a dictionary. Look up words you do not know. Write them in your vocabulary notebook.*

C. *Work with a partner. Take turns reading the diamante poems aloud.*

D. *Discuss these questions with your partner. Write the answers.*

1. Write the word on the first line of each poem. Then write the word on the last line. What do you notice about the first and last lines? Are they synonyms? Are they antonyms (opposites)?

- First word _____

  Last word _____

- First word _____

  Last word _____

- First word _____

  Last word _____

2. What part of speech are the words in line 2? _____

What part of speech are the words in line 6? _____

What do you notice about the words in line 2 and line 6?

_____

3. How are all of the words in lines 3 and 5 similar?

_____

_____

What part of speech are they? _____

What do all the words end in? _____

4. What part of speech are the words in line 4? _____

A. Work with a partner. Write a diamante poem about "happiness" and "sadness."

1. Describe the word *happiness*. Choose two adjectives. Circle them.

> bright   delighted   pleased   sunny

2. Think about the word *happiness*. What actions do you think about? What actions describe your topic? Choose three words. Circle them.

> dancing   jumping   singing   whistling
> dreaming   laughing   smiling

3. Think about nouns that relate to the word *happiness*. Choose two words. Circle them.

> family   friends   joy   sunshine   surprise   warmth

4. Think about nouns that relate to the word *sadness*. Choose two words. Circle them.

> darkness   disappointment   grief   nightmare
> depressed   emptiness   loss   tears

5. Think about the word *sadness*. What actions do you think about? What actions describe the word *sad*? Choose three words. Circle them.

> crying   frowning   missing   weeping
> drowning   hurting   sobbing

6. Describe the word *sadness*. Choose two adjectives. Circle them.

> dark   depressed   gloomy   lonely   miserable

B. **Write your diamante poem on the lines. Use your words in Exercise A.**

Happiness
(first noun – opposite of line 7)

_____ , _____
(adjective)   **(adjective)**

_____ , _____ , _____
(-ing verb)   **(-ing verb)**   **(-ing verb)**

_____ , _____ , _____ , _____ ,
(noun relating to line 1)   **(noun relating to line 1)**   **(noun relating to line 7)**   **(noun relating to line 7)**

_____ , _____ , _____
(-ing verb)   **(-ing verb)**   **(-ing verb)**

_____ , _____
(adjective)   **(adjective)**

_____
(second noun – opposite of line 1)

EXERCISE 6

A. **Write a diamante poem. Follow these steps.**

1. Work with a partner. Read the list of topics for a poem. You can also brainstorm other topics. Remember: Your topic is two nouns that are opposites.

- Noise / Silence
- Day / Night
- Land / Water
- Life / Death
- Winter / Summer
- Spring / Fall
- War / Peace
- Square / Circle

- Child / Adult
- Teacher / Student
- Happiness / Sadness
- Victory / Defeat
- Mountain / Valley
- _____
- _____
- _____

(continued)

2. What is your topic? Write the two nouns. One noun will be the first line of the poem, and the other noun will be the last line.

_____ / _____
(first noun)   (second noun)

3. Think about the first noun. What adjectives describe it? Write adjectives to answer these questions.

- What does it look like? _____

- What color is it? _____

- What does it smell like? Taste like? Sound like? Feel like?

_____

_____

4. What can the first noun do? What actions describe the first noun? (use *-ing* verbs)

_____   _____   _____

5. What are two more nouns that relate to the first noun?

_____   _____

6. Think about the second noun. What are two more nouns that relate to it?

_____   _____

7. What *-ing* verbs can you think of for the second noun?

_____   _____   _____

8. What adjectives describe the second noun?

_____   _____

Remember

Look for *antonyms* and *synonyms* in your dictionary. Many dictionaries list antonyms and synonyms for words. You can also look in an online dictionary.

(See Part 4, Unit 2, for more information about antonyms and synonyms.)

B.   Write your diamante poem on the lines. Use your words in Exercise A.

_____
(first noun – opposite of line 7)

_____ , _____
(adjective)   (adjective)

_____ , _____ , _____
(-*ing* verb)   (-*ing* verb)   (-*ing* verb)

_____ , _____ , _____ , _____ ,
(noun relating to line 1)   (noun relating to line 1)   (noun relating to line 7)   (noun relating to line 7)

_____ , _____ , _____
(-*ing* verb)   (-*ing* verb)   (-*ing* verb)

_____ , _____
(adjective)   (adjective)

_____
(second noun – opposite of line 1)

C.   Share your poem with your class.

WRITING TASK

Write a diamante poem.

**A.   Write a diamante poem with another student or with a small group. Write
your poem on a separate piece of paper.**

B.   Choose one member of your group to read the diamante poem to the class.

Further Practice

Journal or Blog Topic
- Write a cinquain or diamante poem.
- Write a comment about one of your classmate's poems.

Project Idea
- Make a class poetry book.
  - Write or type one or more of your poems. Draw a picture to go
    with your poems.
  - Make enough copies of your poems for everyone in your class.
  - Put all the poems together and make a class poetry book.
  - Design a cover for the class poetry book.

APPENDIX
Grammar and Spelling Guide

VERB TENSES

Simple Present
Affirmative Statements: Regular Verbs

Singular	
Subject	**Verb**
I	play
You	play
He, She, It	plays

Plural	
Subject	**Verb**
We	play
You	play
They	play

Simple Present
Affirmative Statements: *be*

Singular	
Subject	**Verb**
I	am
You	are
He, She, It	is

Plural	
Subject	**Verb**
We	are
You	are
They	are

Simple Present
Negative Statements: Regular Verbs

Singular			
Subject	***do/does***	***not***	**Verb**
I	do	not	play
You	do	not	play
He, She, It	does	not	play

Plural			
Subject	***do/does***	***not***	**Verb**
We	do	not	play
You	do	not	play
They	do	not	play

Simple Present
Negative Statements: *be*

Singular			
Subject	***be***	***not***	
I	am	not	late
You	are	not	late
He, She, It	is	not	late

Plural			
Subject	***be***	***not***	
We	are	not	late
You	are	not	late
They	are	not	late

Simple Past
Affirmative Statements: Regular Verbs

Singular	
Subject	**Verb**
I	played
You	played
He, She, It	played

Plural	
Subject	**Verb**
We	played
You	played
They	played

Simple Past
Affirmative Statements: *be*

Singular	
Subject	**Verb**
I	was
You	were
He, She, It	was

Plural	
Subject	**Verb**
We	were
You	were
They	were

Simple Past
Negative Statements: Regular Verbs

Singular			
Subject	***did***	***not***	**Verb**
I	did	not	play
You	did	not	play
He, She, It	did	not	play

Plural			
Subject	***did***	***not***	**Verb**
We	did	not	play
You	did	not	play
They	did	not	play

Simple Past
Negative Statements: *be*

Singular			
Subject	***be***	***not***	
I	was	not	late
You	were	not	late
He, She, It	was	not	late

Plural			
Subject	***be***	***not***	
We	were	not	late
You	were	not	late
They	were	not	late

Present Progressive
Affirmative Statements

Singular		
Subject	***be***	**Verb + *ing***
I	am	playing
You	are	playing
He, She, It	is	playing

Plural		
Subject	***Be***	**Verb + *ing***
We	are	playing
You	are	playing
They	are	playing

Present Progressive
Negative Statements

Singular			
Subject	***be***	***not***	**Verb + *ing***
I	am	not	playing
You	are	not	playing
He, She, It	is	not	playing

Plural			
Subject	***be***	***not***	**Verb + *ing***
We	are	not	playing
You	are	not	playing
They	are	not	playing

SPELLING RULES

Simple Present Singular Verbs with *He*, *She*, and *It*

1. For most verbs, add the letter "s" to the base form of the verb
   Examples: *play – plays*   *walk – walks*   *write – writes*

2. For verbs that end in "-sh", "-ch", "-ss", "x", add "-es"
   Examples: *rush – rushes*   *watch – watches*   *fix – fixes*

3. For verbs that end in a consonant + "y", change "y" to "i" and then add "-es"
   Examples: *fly – flies*   *try – tries*   *carry – carries*

Adding *-ing*

1. For most verbs, add "-ing" to the base form of the verb
   Examples: *play – playing   jump – jumping   go – going*

2. For verbs that end in "e" drop the final "-e" and add "-ing"
   Examples: *leave – leaving   make – making   receive – receiving*

3. For most verbs that end in consonant-vowel-consonant (CVC) combination, double the last consonant and then add "-ing"
   Examples: *sit – sitting   run – running   begin – beginning*

4. For verbs that end in "ie" change the "ie" to "y" then add "-ing"
   Examples: *die – dying   lie – lying*

Exceptions:

1. Do <u>not</u> double the last consonant in verbs that end in "w", "x", or "y"
   Examples: *sew – sewing   fix – fixing   enjoy – enjoying*

2. Do <u>not</u> double the last consonant if the last syllable of a verb is not stressed
   Examples: *happen – happening   listen – listening*

Simple Past of Regular Verbs

1. For most verbs, add "-ed" to the base form of the verb
   Examples: *play – played   jump – jumped*

2. For verbs that end in "e," add "-d" to the end.
   Examples: *hope – hoped   love – loved   save – saved*

3. For most verbs that end in consonant-vowel-consonant (CVC) combination, double the last consonant and then add "-ed"
   Examples: *stop – stopped   plan – planned   beg – begged*

4. For verbs that end in consonant + "y", drop the "y" and add "-ied"
   Examples: *study – studied   hurry – hurried   try – tried*

Exceptions:

1. Do <u>not</u> double the last consonant in verbs that end in "w", "x", or "y"
   Examples: *sew – sewed   fix – fixed   enjoy – enjoyed*

2. Do <u>not</u> double the last consonant if the last syllable of a verb is not stressed
   Examples: *happen – happened   listen – listened*

Simple Past Irregular Verbs

Base Form	Simple Past
be	was, were
become	became
begin	began
bend	bent
bite	bit
blow	blew
break	broke
bring	brought
build	built
buy	bought
catch	caught
choose	chose
come	came
cost	cost
cut	cut
do	did
draw	drew
drive	drove
drink	drank
eat	ate
fall	fell
feel	felt
fight	fought
find	found
fly	flew
forget	forgot
forgive	forgave
get	got
give	gave
go	went
grow	grew
have	had
hear	heard
hide	hid
hit	hit
hold	held

Base Form	Simple Past
hurt	hurt
keep	kept
know	knew
leave	left
let	let
lose	lost
make	made
meet	met
pay	paid
put	put
read	read
ride	rode
ring	rang
run	ran
say	said
see	saw
sell	sold
send	sent
shut	shut
sing	sang
sit	sat
sleep	slept
speak	spoke
spend	spent
stand	stood
swim	swam
take	took
teach	taught
tell	told
think	thought
throw	threw
understand	understood
wake	woke
wear	wore
win	won
write	wrote

CAPITALIZATION RULES

Rule	Examples
Use a capital letter . . .	
For the pronoun *I*	*Maria and I are roommates.* *Janet knows where I live.*
At the beginning of every sentence	*The people in my class are friendly.* *We usually have lunch together.*
For the names of people and their titles	*I have an appointment with Dr. Friedman.* *My teacher's name is Mr. Davis.*
For the names of places such as countries, cities, continents, states, rivers, mountains, oceans, and so on	*Dallas, Texas* *South America* *Seoul, Korea* *Pacific Ocean* *the Nile River*
For the names of nationalities, religions, languages	*British, Thai* *Christianity, Islam, Buddhism, Judaism* *Japanese, Spanish, English*
For the month of the year, days of the week, and holidays (do not capitalize the names of seasons: spring, summer, fall, winter)	*June* *Ramadan* *Thursday* *Thanksgiving* *New Year's Day*
For the first word of a greeting and closing in letters and emails	*Dear Mom and Dad,* *Sincerely,*
For the names of organizations, schools, and companies	*The United Nations* *Stanford University, Dartmouth College* *Microsoft*
For the names of buildings, streets, structures, bridges	*Sears Tower* *Taj Mahal* *Locust Street* *Brooklyn Bridge*
For the first, last, and any important word in the title of a book, magazine, newspaper, song, movie, poem, or other work. (Do not capitalize prepositions, articles, or conjunctions unless they are the first word.)	*A Tale of Two Cities* *Titanic* *Pride and Prejudice* *National Geographic* *The Post Standard*

PUNCTUATION RULES

Punctuation Mark	Uses	Examples
Period	• Use a period at the end of a sentence.	*We enjoyed the concert.*
	• Use a period after an initial.	*My favorite poet is T. S. Elliot.*
	• Use a period after an abbreviation.	*Mrs. Rudolph is an excellent teacher.*
	• Use a period to separate dollars and cents.	*These shoes cost $79.95.*
Exclamation Point	Use an exclamation point at the end of a sentence, phrase, or word to show surprise or strong emotion.	*Wow!* *Slow down!* *That sounds great!*
Question Mark	Use a question mark at the end of a question.	*Are you going to the movie with us?*
Comma	• Use a comma between the date and the year.	*January 9, 2013*
	• Use a comma after the greeting and closing in a letter or email.	*Dear Janet,* *Best Wishes,*
	• Use a comma between the city and the state in an address.	*Miami, Florida*
	• Use a comma after an introductory word or phrase at the beginning of a sentence.	*Suddenly, the rain stopped.* *After that, peel the carrots.*
	• Use a comma after each item in a series of three or more items.	*I need to buy lettuce, tomatoes, onions, and peas.*
	• Use a comma after the first part of a compound sentence.	*I was tired, so I took a nap.*
	• Use a comma after a dependent clause when it comes first in a sentence.	*After the movie, we went for a walk.*
	• Use a comma in large numbers. Counting from right to left, use a comma after every 3 digits. (Do not use a comma in writing years.)	*The population of Havertown was 25,677 in 2012.*

Colon	• Use a colon after the greeting of a business letter.	*Dear Professor Brown:*
	• Use a colon between the hour and the seconds.	*The movie starts at 8:30.*
Apostrophe	• Use an apostrophe in a contraction to show where a letter(s) is left out.	*I'm sorry we're late.*
	• Use an apostrophe to form a possessive noun.	*Gary's car is in the garage.*
Quotation Marks	Use quotation marks before and after a direct quote (the speaker's exact words).	*Harris said, "Lock the door when you leave."*

Credits

Photo Credits

All photos are used under license from Shutterstock.com except for the following: **Page 16 (bottom)** Dreamstime.com; **p. 62 (b)** i love images/Alamy; **p. 145** ZUMA Press/Newscom; **p. 152** Royalty-Free/Corbis/Glow Images; **p. 179** Jeffrey Coolidge/Corbis; **p. 214 (left)** Gallo Images/Alamy, **(right)** ImagineGolf/ iStockphoto.com; **p. 228 (left)** mauritius images GmbH/Alamy; **p. 241** Everett Collection Inc/Alamy.